THE MAKING OF A ROOKIE

What does a player go through in his first year in the N.F.L.? How is he chosen in the college draft? What are his chances of making the team? What happens if he is seriously injured? Howard Liss answers these and many other questions by examining the rookie careers of four young players who have proved their ability to compete with the best pro football has to offer. They are: Gale Sayers, Jim Hart, Bubba Smith and Paul Warfield.

THE MAKING OF A ROOKIE

by HOWARD LISS

Illustrated with photographs

Glossary of pro football terms

RANDOM HOUSE
NEW YORK

Library of Congress Catalog Card Number: 68-26887

Manufactured in the United States of America

For ERNIE DAVIS, *who*
surely would have been
a great rookie

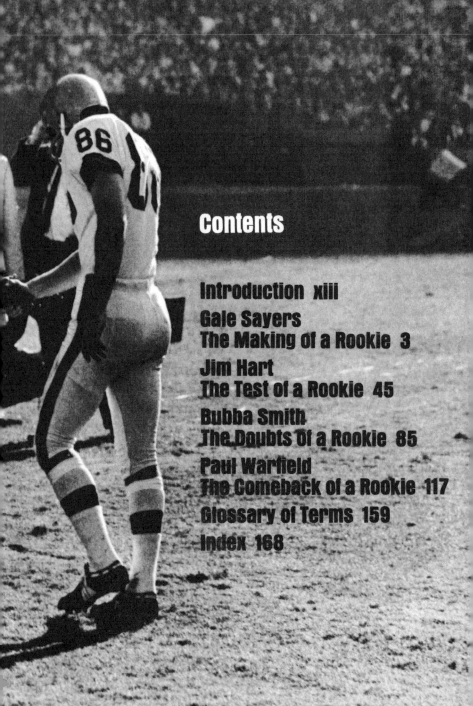

Contents

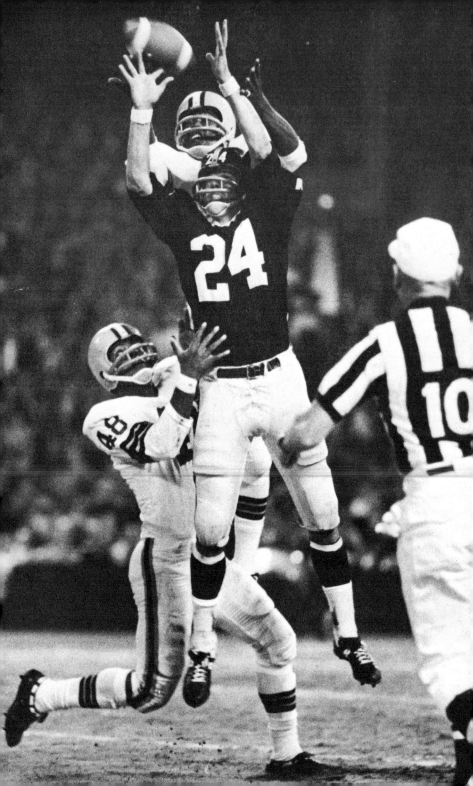

Introduction

On September 5, 1967, 111 pro football players lost their jobs. Some were eager young rookies who had been outstanding college players. They had gone to training camp confident that they could make the team, but found they weren't good enough. Others were veterans who had been unable to beat back the challenge of stronger and faster newcomers.

Those who remained could be sure of only one thing—some day it would happen to them, too. Every player knew in his heart that it was only a question of time before a rookie came along who had the power, the speed or the throwing arm to take away the veteran's place on the club.

Rookies are the lifeblood of every professional sport. Even the greatest stars last only a comparatively few years, and eventually new players come along to replace them. And many of those players become stars in their own right. During summer practice the coaches cast a critical eye on the crop of fledgling hopefuls, trying to determine who will be given a spot on the team and who will be dropped after the training season.

The coaches do not always choose wisely. For example, a young man named Lionel Taylor went to the Chicago Bears' training camp from tiny New Mexico Highlands College, trying to earn a berth at end. He didn't make it. Still trying to find a niche for himself in pro football, Taylor tried out with the Denver Broncos of the American Football League, and there he found a home. Strong, aggressive, with sure hands and the ability to outjump defensive halfbacks, Taylor became an All-League receiver.

On the other hand, some players with a "can't miss" label never make the grade. If they do manage to become members of a pro team, they usually never rise above the rank of substitute and eventually drop out when better rookies arrive.

Sometimes a star is so great that no rookie, however talented, can take away his position. When Y. A. Tittle was throwing the football for the San Francisco 49ers, he was challenged by a prize rookie almost every year. First it was Jim Powers of U.S.C., and then came Maury Duncan of San Francisco State, Earl Morrall of Michigan State and John Brodie of Stanford. They all tried to oust the veteran quarterback from the number-one spot, and all failed. Brodie was able to win the place in the starting line-up only after Tittle was injured.

There are many factors that determine a rookie's fate. He must be fortunate enough to avoid injury during training and exhibition games, for he is not likely to have many opportunities to show his skills. He must learn quickly, for professional offensive and defensive assignments are more difficult to master than those in college. And he must have "desire"—that is, the courage, determination and perseverance to overcome all obstacles that stand between him and a place in the starting line-up.

The careers of four rookies are presented in this book. They have met with varying degrees of success in their first years as pro football players. But all have proved one point—they have been good enough to play against the top competition in the country.

THE MAKING OF A ROOKIE

THE MAKING OF A ROOKIE
GALE SAYERS

More than 43,000 fans at Chicago's Wrigley Field were on their feet, filling the football stadium with the sound of a roaring chant: "WE WANT SAYERS!" The Bears had the ball on the San Francisco 49ers' two-yard line, and the crowd was calling for Gale Sayers to come off the bench, grab the pigskin and slice in for the touchdown. That would break the pro football record for touchdowns scored by one player in a single game. For "The Kansas Tornado" had already scored six touchdowns in the contest.

Sayers leaps over San Francisco's goal line during the third period to score one of his six touchdowns that day.

Early in the first period, Sayers had taken a screen pass from quarterback Rudy Bukich, wriggled away from enemy tacklers and raced 80 yards for his first touchdown. In the second quarter he had scored twice more, once on a 21-yard end sweep and again on a seven-yard sprint around end. In the third period he had taken a pitchout from the quarterback and loped 50 yards into the end zone. Again in the third period he had gone over the goal line, this time on a one-yard power plunge through the middle of the line. In the fourth quarter he had fielded a punt on his own 15-yard line, sped up the middle, cut to the sidelines and run away from everybody to score touchdown number six.

Only two other players in history had scored six times in one game. On Thanksgiving Day, 1929, the immortal Ernie Nevers, playing with the old Chicago Cardinals, had achieved the feat. On November 25, 1951, Dub Jones of the Cleveland Browns had run for four touchdowns and scored twice more on passes.

Now, on December 12, 1965, Gale Sayers of the Chicago Bears, the rookie known for his blazing speed, had a chance to break that record. Surely, with the help of the inspired Chicago forward wall, he could manage to get across the final chalk stripe.

But Sayers never scored his seventh touchdown. He stayed on the bench, huddled in his parka, and watched veteran halfback Jon Arnett plunge into the end zone. Later, sportswriters asked Head Coach George "Papa Bear" Halas why he had not allowed his rookie sensation to try for one more score.

"Nobody was hungrier than I was to have Sayers score number seven," Halas replied. "But we had it cinched already. What if he'd been hurt? I'd never forgive myself. He's a fine boy."

Sayers agreed with the strategy of his head coach. Nor was he overly disappointed. "It wouldn't have done me any good," he pointed out. "The 49ers knew the game was lost. If I'd come back they would have known why I was on the field and they'd have been ready for me. Leaving Arnett in was a good move. He scored, didn't he?"

As the sportswriters started to leave, one of them stated flatly that Gale Sayers was as good as, if not better than, Cleveland's great Jimmy Brown.

"No," said Sayers softly but firmly. "I'm no Jimmy Brown."

Perhaps the record-tying performance was fated to happen, for Gale Sayers had been playing football for 14 years before his rookie season with the Bears. He had started in the fourth grade at grammar school and had excelled even then. In the seventh and eighth grades, playing "midget football," he scored 21 touchdowns in nine games. He was already showing flashes of his future greatness by the time he entered high school.

At Omaha Central High Gale really blossomed out, not only in football but in track and field as well. Speed seemed to run in the Sayers' family. (Strangely enough, Gale spent part of his boyhood on a farm just outside the town of Speed, Kansas.) His older brother, Roger, was a sprinter and had once beaten Bob Hayes in a dual meet before the latter went on to become an Olympic champion.

Gale made the track team easily, but later he encountered some difficulty keeping ahead of his teammates.

"What's the trouble?" athletic coach Frank Smagacz asked the gangly youngster. "I thought you were going to be the fastest man we ever had here."

The boy grinned shyly. "Coach," he said, "I've grown two-and-a-half inches in the last few months. I guess my speed didn't keep up with me."

Even as a high-school athlete Sayers showed that he had the will to win. In one track meet he was tied in the broad-jump event with a boy from Lincoln, Nebraska. Both had leaped 22 feet 4 inches. "I'll settle this!" Gale said. And on the final try he jumped 22 feet 6½ inches.

Later, when Sayers was with the Bears, Coach Smagacz analyzed his former pupil's ability to break away from tacklers.

"When Gale was a senior Omaha Central won the state football and track championships," he noted. "Gale took the title in the hurdles and broad jump. It was the jumping experience that made him a great football runner. Not only did he develop a great change of pace that made him

Sayers as a high-school broad jumper.

elusive, hard to grab and hold, but also, because his knees rose higher than his hips when he ran, he had great spring to go with his speed."

In spite of his success in track-and-field sports, football was always the youngster's primary interest. He became a regular in his sophomore year, shining on offense and defense. His position was right halfback, and he made himself a greater threat by learning how to pass well, too. The fact that he threw the ball left-handed made him doubly dangerous. For all defensive players are accustomed to right-handed passers and are taken by surprise when a southpaw suddenly throws the ball. This was another skill which was to stand him in good stead when he reached the pros.

Yet, in spite of instant stardom, which has inflated the egos of many college players, Gale was never a disciplinary problem for his coaches. In fact, he was usually the first man on the field, practicing the moves that were to astonish pro football's defenses. Once, while playing against Omaha Benson High, he took a pitchout and swept to his right. The defense shifted over to meet him. Gale shifted, too. Before anyone knew what was happening he had streaked to his left and was running down the sidelines all by himself.

Coach Smagacz was able to see another of Sayers' touchdown runs only on film. During that game, West Side High School had driven deep inside Omaha Central territory, but then their attack stalled. On the fourth down, with only one yard to go for a first down, West Side decided to try a quick pass. But the ball was thrown wide, and Coach Smagacz turned to tell his offensive unit to get into the ball game. Instead of obeying, the players laughed. Turning back, the coach saw that Sayers, who had been playing in the linebacker spot, had intercepted the errant pass and had gone all the way for a touchdown!

While in high school, Gale picked up the nickname "Pookie" from his frequent visits to a "Pookieburger" stand near the school. The stand gave away free sandwiches to every player who scored a touchdown. Of course, Gale led everybody else in acquiring free Pookieburgers.

The young man from Omaha Central High expected to receive a flood of offers from colleges and universities when he was graduated in 1961. He was not disappointed. He was contacted by more than 75 schools, including U.C.L.A., Notre Dame, Big-Eight and Big-Ten schools, plus many others. All his friends expected him to pick Nebraska. Since he lived in Omaha and had been an All-Nebraska halfback, it seemed only natural that he would attend the state university at Lincoln. To everyone's surprise, he chose to attend Kansas University.

When Sayers announced his decision, Nebraska fans were outraged. One local sportswriter stated in his column, "It seems that Gale Sayers is out to get as much as he can!"

If the young athlete was hurt by that remark he did not let it show. In a way, however, the accusation was true. Gale had made up his mind to play pro football, and he was preparing for it just as carefully as anyone else would prepare for a different career. He had two basic reasons for choosing Kansas:

First, Kansas had a better football record than Nebraska at the time, and Gale realized that he could attract more attention from the pros if he was with one of the top college teams. Second, he liked Coach Jack Mitchell and felt that Mitchell could teach him a great deal about football.

Sayers had made many other plans, too. And not all of them pertained to football. During his senior year at high school he had met a pretty girl named Linda McNeil, who attended one of Omaha Central's rival schools. Linda didn't know much about football, but she did like Gale, even though he was a shy, sensitive, quiet sort of fellow whose idea of a good time was to sit around and listen to good jazz music. He neither drank nor smoked, and didn't care to attend parties. It wasn't that he was unfriendly or "the strong, silent type." Music had always been one of his hobbies. Later, when he was starring for the Bears and was being interviewed by sportswriters in his home, Gale would sometimes get so interested in the music coming from his tape recorder that he would forget to answer questions.

Gale and Linda were married after his freshman year in college, and he is the first to admit that it was one of the best things he has ever done. Not only did Linda prove to be a steadying influence and help him with his studies, but she also contributed to the family finances by working in a stationery store and by part-time modeling in nearby Kansas City.

Starting with his freshman year, Sayers began to live up to all his advance notices. In two games against arch-rival Kansas State, he scored seven touchdowns for the freshman team. And every spare moment was spent in practice and more practice under the watchful eye of Coach Mitchell. The varsity mentor did not want his young charge to become just another speed demon. Instead, he stressed control and balance, the skills so necessary for a football player to have.

Halfback Sayers runs around right end as two Boston University tacklers close in on him.

Mitchell's coaching paid off. Sayers played in 30 straight games, although the string was almost snapped during his sophomore year. Gale had injured his hand and wasn't quite sure he'd be fit to play. The coach and his halfback talked over the situation, and Sayers decided to give it a try. His performance amounted to more than just a try, for that afternoon he scored five touchdowns and gained more than 300 yards.

At K.U. Sayers' ball carrying and the fakes he used against enemy tacklers are still a topic of conversation. In one game against Oklahoma he took the kickoff near his own goal line, raced up-field and swerved away from a swarm of opposing defensive men. Only one Oklahoma player stood in his path, and he seemed to have the speedy Kansan dead in his sights. But Sayers was determined not to be stopped. He faked with his head, his shoulders, his hips, with his whole body. As the crowd gaped in amazement, the Oklahoma tackler became so confused that he fell to his knees and allowed the Kansas Tornado to race right by him for a touchdown!

Sayers played against Nebraska only once during his college career. Some people thought he was taking his life in his hands by venturing out on the field. Nebraska fans had not forgiven him for supposedly snubbing their university, and the Cornhuskers were set to do violence to the fleet halfback if they could lay their hands on him. But matters didn't work out that way. In fact, Sayers set a record against Nebraska that day.

The Cornhuskers' attack had sputtered and stalled at midfield, and their punter, aiming at the coffin corner, booted the ball out of bounds on the Kansas one-foot line. The Huskers lined up shoulder to shoulder, ready to swoop in and overwhelm the ball carrier for a two-point safety.

The Kansas quarterback, noting the stacked forward wall, decided to take a daring gamble. He reasoned that a power plunge wouldn't get very far because it would be too tough to wedge an opening in the defense. A pass was too risky because there wasn't much room to maneuver, and the quarterback took a risk of being brought down in his end zone. Only one possible type of play remained—a quick end sweep by his fastest man, Gale Sayers. That was the play he called in the huddle.

Sayers was moving with the snap of the ball and the big Nebraska line came charging straight ahead. He took the quarterback's quick toss, picked up a key block, turned the corner and was in the open. It was the longest touchdown run of his college career, measuring exactly 99 yards and two feet!

It is no wonder that Gale Sayers was chosen for All-America honors during his last two years in college and was called the greatest back ever to come out of the Big-Eight Conference. A look at the statistics proves his greatness.

During his three-year varsity career at Kansas, his rushing total was 2,675 yards, averaging out to 6.5 yards per carry. He caught 35 passes good for 408 yards, returned 22 kickoffs 513 yards and 28 punts for 324 yards. But those are merely his personal statistics. It would be impossible to figure out how often the K.U. quarterback completed his passes or other ball carriers gained yardage simply because the defenses were chasing Sayers when he didn't have the ball.

At Kansas Sayers was accustomed to making headlines on the sports pages of newspapers, but he once made the papers for an incident that did not concern football. It showed that the young star was interested in more important things than sports and that the welfare of his fellow Negroes was of great concern to him.

In March, 1965, during his senior year, Gale and his wife took part in a sit-in demonstration against segregation of housing at the University. Both were arrested and placed in jail. They were released after three hours, but Gale was so angry that he did not care if he was suspended from college or not. It was a long time before he was able to talk about the incident calmly.

The demonstration had not been composed of Negroes alone. Of the 113 students who had been arrested, 75 were white and only 38 Negro. Nor was Sayers protesting about his own living conditions, which were very good. But others of his race were forced to live in poor quarters, and his conscience could not tolerate such inequality. As he put it, "They accept me as a football star, but not as a Negro."

Throughout his college career, Sayers had

been scouted by the pros. A number of clubs wanted him, but two were particularly interested in obtaining his services—the Chicago Bears and the Kansas City Chiefs. The report of the Chicago scouts was especially flattering. It said of Sayers: "Halfback, great speed, great prospect. Should be graded in the 'one' category."

But there was one aspect of Sayers' play that was not so flattering. A number of coaches who had seen him in action thought that he could not —or would not—do any blocking. Both Sayers and Jack Mitchell thought that such criticism was unfair. Mitchell in particular defended his star graduate, saying that Sayers could block as well as any college halfback in the country and was as good as some in the pro ranks.

Besides, a number of coaches, including a few who were in charge of professional teams, claimed that a man like Gale Sayers did not have to block all the time. In fact, sometimes it was better if he didn't. The idea behind blocking, they pointed out, was to get one or more defensive men out of the way so that they could not upset an offensive maneuver. There would always be a couple of defenders—a linebacker and a corner halfback—"keyed in" on Sayers, following him wherever he went, regardless of whether he had the ball or not. Therefore, he was taking a couple of men out of the way and wasn't risking injury by trying to block out a heavy defensive player. Of course, Sayers had to block part of the time, but there were few who thought he wouldn't measure up in that department.

Regardless of any faults he had, the Bears wanted him, but were afraid he was out of reach. They had the third pick in the annual draft. The New York Giants and San Francisco 49ers were ahead of them. So the Bears held their breath and waited. The Giants chose a fine running back named Tucker Frederickson, and San Francisco picked another good back named Ken Willard. As a result, the Bears were able to draft Sayers. But their problems weren't over. They still had to contend with the Kansas City Chiefs of the American Football League.

The Chiefs had a very good chance to sign Sayers. They pointed out that he would be playing before Kansas City fans, who had followed him during his entire college career. They were his "home folks." In addition, Texas millionaire Lamar Hunt, owner of the Chiefs, offered a large amount of money as an inducement.

In the Bears' behalf, Coach Halas sent Claude "Buddy" Young to talk to Sayers. Young had played for the Baltimore Colts and had been a star himself. Sayers listened to both offers and finally decided to sign a contract with Chicago.

He was now a pro football player. But there was still one amateur game left on his schedule. He had been selected for the college All-Star team, which would play against the N.F.L. champions, the Cleveland Browns.

Before reporting for the All-Star contest, Sayers went through a workout with the Bears at their training camp. During the first scrimmage, he suddenly limped off the field, claiming that he had injured his leg. Taking no chances with his prize rookie, Halas had him examined by the team physician, who could find nothing wrong. But Sayers insisted that he had been hurt.

When Otto Graham, coach of the All-Star squad, heard of the incident, he thought Sayers was faking the injured leg to get out of playing in the game. "This boy Sayers has as great a talent as any athlete I've seen," Graham said angrily, "but he'll never make it with the Bears unless he changes his attitude, because Halas won't have him."

By game time Gale wanted to play, but Coach Graham refused to send him in. "I guess," said the halfback later, "by that time Graham was really convinced I was goofing off."

George Halas, however, believed that Sayers might well have been injured and used the rookie sparingly in the first two exhibition games.

If there was a turning point in the professional football career of Gale Sayers, it was the third exhibition game of the season, which was played in Nashville against the Los Angeles Rams. What he showed was enough to convince everybody that he could become the most exciting ball carrier in the National Football League. Among other things, he ran back a punt for 77 yards and his first pro touchdown; he ran 93 yards with a kickoff; he caught a pass good for 25 yards. Then he topped off his performance with a fancy left-handed scoring pass to teammate Jim Jones.

The Bears were particularly delighted with Gale's passing ability. Now they had a real threat, for they could use the halfback option-play with deadly effect. This called for Sayers to take a hand-off or pitchout and sweep toward the sidelines. If the corner linebacker and corner halfback charged forward to tackle him, he could throw a pass to an end or flanker, who could slip into open territory. If the defensive men dropped back to cover the pass, Sayers could simply tuck the ball under his arm and keep running, usually for a good gain.

In spite of Gale's outstanding work against the Rams, the Bears kept their rookie under wraps through the remainder of the exhibition season

Gale Sayers arches a pass over the heads of Viking defenders.

and the first two regular-season games against the 49ers and the Rams, both of which they lost. Then, with the fearsome Green Bay Packers as their next opponent, the Chicago coach knew the time had come to put his new halfback into the starting line-up.

The Bears didn't win that game either, but when it was over, they knew they had the potential to become a winning ball club. The final score was Green Bay 23, Chicago 14. Gale Sayers had scored both Bear touchdowns, one on a run, the other on a 65-yard pass play.

Now firmly installed as the starting halfback, Gale led the Bears to a revenge victory over the

Rams. Once again he was responsible for two touchdowns. He scored one after catching a screen pass and running 80 yards. Then he tossed a 26-yard pass to end Dick Gordon to account for the other.

During those games and throughout the season, Bear coaches watched every move the rookie made and began to find a few flaws in his play. First, he was "jitterbugging" too much—that is, he was waiting too long to make his move once he had the ball. A player with his incredible speed should have been hitting the hole in the line quicker or reaching the sidelines faster and turning the corner.

Second, he had a tendency to follow his blockers too closely—to "run up their backs," so to speak.

Gale also had to learn to adjust to the quarterback's "audibles." Sometimes, after a play had been decided on in the huddle, the quarterback might suddenly change it at the line of scrimmage when he noticed an opening in the defense. This was done by calling out different numbers in a loud voice. But Gale was concentrating so hard on his own assignment that he often seemed not to hear the new signals.

After a while, Sayers began to learn that pro football players have a kind of instinct when it came to blocking. He saw that this was especially true on kick-offs. No matter where the ball went, they seemed to know how to set themselves quickly, form a pattern and carry out their assignments. The rest was up to the ball carrier.

The rookie also found out quickly that the pros were bigger, heavier and hit much harder than college players. Yet he seemed to shrug off even the defensive giants when they piled into him. On Sayers' 80-yard sprint against the Rams, Chuck Lamson had caught him around the waist, but Gale had swivel-hipped away. Then Roosevelt Grier, who stood 6 feet 5 inches tall and weighed 285 pounds, crashed into him.

"I thought I hit him so hard that he fumbled," said Grier later. "But he didn't. When I looked up he was already 15 yards past me, heading for the touchdown."

One thing Sayers never had to learn from the pros was that football is a team game. He had learned that a long time ago. Even in high school, after he had scored a touchdown or made a long gain, he always congratulated the linemen and complimented the blockers who had made the gain possible.

He was faking better than ever, too. On his six-yard touchdown sweep against Green Bay, he had faked five times before he ran two yards.

Sayers snares a pass during a game with Minnesota.

Some runners would have lost valuable time, but not Gale. He was moving forward during his fakes.

In game number four, against the Minnesota Vikings, Sayers' performance reinforced the belief among the other teams in the N.F.L. that they were in for trouble whenever the Bear halfback was on the field. For most of the game the Vikings had managed to keep the Kansas Tornado away from their goal line. Then, with 40 seconds left in the third quarter, Sayers caught an 18-yard pass from quarterback Rudy Bukich, wrenched free from the clutches of a pair of defensive backs at the five-yard line and went in to score.

That was just a warm-up for the action to come. Early in the fourth period he caught another touchdown pass from Bukich, which covered 25 yards. And then, as the game pounded into its climactic moments, Sayers executed the play that Viking coach Norm Van Brocklin had been afraid of throughout the game.

Minnesota had just scored to take a 37-31 lead over the Bears. Only two-and-a-half minutes were left in the game. With Sayers standing back on his goal line ready to receive, Minnesota kicker Fred Cox received specific orders from his coach: he was to boot the ball high and far, right out of the stadium if necessary, but above all he was to keep it away from Sayers. Cox tried to oblige, but the wind held up the ball and Sayers was able to grab it at the four-yard line on a dead run.

The fleet Chicago ball-carrier swung to the sideline and then headed for the open field. Only the safetyman and two defensive halfbacks had a chance to stop him, but Sayers faked them out with his shoulder as he streaked away for a 96-yard touchdown run.

Characteristically, he gave full credit to his blocking. Yet, when Gale had reached the Viking 20-yard line, he had turned to look back over his shoulder. As he explained later, "I was in the clear and didn't want anyone to throw a block be-

Sayers weaves through a tangle of Viking defenders.

cause I was afraid they might call a clipping penalty and nullify the run. I was just telling my blockers to back off."

Gale put the finishing touches on his performance with a 10-yard drive through a hole up the middle, running over two defensemen and into the end zone. It was his fourth touchdown of the day. Earlier, he had almost been responsible for another score, which would have given him five touchdowns.

The Bears had called for the option pass. Gale had taken the hand-off, but as he was moving out he slipped and fell. Still, he managed to get up and complete the pass to teammate Dick Gordon, and the play covered 27 yards. It could have produced a touchdown, for Gordon had beaten his man by a step or two, but when Sayers fell down Gordon was forced to come back to catch the pass. As a result, he was tackled before he reached the end zone.

It wasn't long before the rest of the league began to zero in on Sayers. In a game against the Lions he was stopped cold on a kickoff return. Detroit's Wally Hillenberg hit him so hard with a diving tackle that it took Gale a few minutes to regain his senses.

Yet he shrugged it off. "Most of the time they grab my legs or jersey and throw me down," he said. "If they ever hit me solidly, I'll be out of there!"

The Baltimore Colts were the next team to successfully stop the great rookie. They covered him so closely that they were able to bottle him up and hold his rushing to a total of 17 yards in 11 attempts. Gale spent most of the second half on the sidelines. He did, however, manage to accumulate 41 yards in pass receptions and 71 more on kickoff returns. Later in the game he almost scored when he raced downfield and outran everybody while trying to catch up with a long pass from Bukich that narrowly missed.

The loss to Baltimore turned out to be the sort

of bad game that every player experiences now and then. Sayers just had to get it out of his system. He soon had the Bears back on the winning track. His fantastic speed and incredible fakes were rapidly becoming the talk of the pro football world.

Against the St. Louis Cardinals, Gale caught a kickoff on his one-yard line, cut to his right and slipped away from two tacklers as he headed for the sideline. At the 30-yard line he found himself facing the kicker, Jim Bakken. Gale cut back inside and raced all the way to the St. Louis 13-yard line, where he was finally caught from behind. "He was winded from all that running," George Halas explained. "That man was moving all over the field, otherwise they never would have caught him."

In the fourth quarter of that game Gale scored on a seven-yard run up the middle. Four Cardinals had a chance to stop him. They all missed.

Later, Chicago upset the mighty Green Bay Packers by a score of 31-10. In that game he raced 66 yards for one touchdown, and sprinted 10 yards for another. His 62-yard punt return set up a third Chicago score.

"That kid is the greatest to come into the league in my time," remarked Packer star Paul Hornung after the game.

Sayers sprints through a gap in the Packer defense.

Green Bay coach Vince Lombardi was equally generous in his praise of the Bears' halfback. "Sayers can be a great one," he said.

Gale made the option pass a nightmare for the New York Giants. The first time he tried, he threw a beauty that was caught in the end zone. But the play was called back because of a holding penalty against one of the Bears. However, the first pass paid off because the next time he moved into the flat zone he merely lifted his arm and the whole Giant defense dropped back. So Gale kept the ball and raced 45 yards for the score.

Later, he tried the same play again. By that time the bewildered Giants didn't know what to expect. As they stood momentarily frozen, Gale lobbed the ball to his receiver for the touchdown.

Sayers scored twice in that game, and in doing so he broke two records. His total of 14 touchdowns broke the rookie record of 13 set by Green Bay's Billy Howton in 1953. He also broke the Chicago club record of 12 set by Rick Casares in 1956. And the season wasn't over!

The next game was against Baltimore, and the Bears had a score to settle. This time the Colts found it impossible to stop Sayers, no matter how they dogged his footsteps. The final score was Chicago 13, Baltimore 0.

In one crucial play it seemed at first that Gale

would be trapped behind the line of scrimmage for a three-yard loss. But while the Bears' right tackle took out defensive end Lou Michaels, Gale simply outmaneuvered defenseman Bob Boyd and galloped 61 yards for the score.

Then came Sayers' magnificent six-touchdown afternoon against the 49ers. The first five times he crossed the goal line, Gale simply flipped the ball to the referee and trotted off the field. But the sixth time was different. As he raced into the end zone he flung the football high into the air and danced away clapping his hands. Seconds later he was mobbed by his teammates, who lifted him off the ground, pounded him on the back and wrung his hand. Later, they broke tradition by awarding him the game ball for the second time that season. Nobody on the Bears had ever received that honor before.

Papa Bear Halas joined the festivities. "Red Grange, George McAfee, Gale Sayers," he roared, naming three of the greatest ball carriers ever to wear the Chicago uniform. "And not necessarily in the order named!"

Besides Gale's sixth touchdown, there was one other play in the game that brought him great satisfaction, even though the newspapers didn't give it all the attention it deserved. The play occurred during the second quarter, when the Bears

Trailing a line of tacklers, Sayers lunges through the

Giant defense.

were leading by a relatively slim 13-7 margin.

The 49ers' attack had bogged down, so punter Tommy Davis kicked the ball deep into Bear territory. Sayers and Jon Arnett were playing back. Davis had the good sense to keep the ball away from Sayers. Arnett took the ball on his own two-yard line and got up a full head of steam. At the 40-yard line, the 49ers' rugged Jerry Mertens came chugging up to make the tackle. But he never reached Arnett because Sayers hit him with a slashing block, allowing Arnett to break loose all the way to the San Francisco 21-yard line. This was Sayers' answer to the critics who said he couldn't block.

In the final game of the season the Bears took on the Minnesota Vikings, and Gale had a chance to win the league rushing championship. He made an all-out effort and played a brilliant game. He carried the ball 19 times for an amazing total of 197 yards, which gave him a combined total of 1,271 yards for the year—well over the figure needed to win the title. He beat Leroy Kelly of the Cleveland Browns by 90 yards and became the first halfback to win the rushing title since the great Steve Van Buren in 1949.

In that last game Sayers also received the first real bruises of his pro football career. During the first period, Viking punter Bobby Walden lofted a high pass into the December sky and Gale gathered it in. Unfortunately, it had never occurred to him to signal for a fair catch, and as he looked up he saw half of the Viking team staring down his throat. They gang-tackled him and drove him back for a six-yard loss.

"I don't remember who they were, but two, three, maybe four of 'em got me," Gale grinned ruefully. "Somebody got his arm—or something —through my face mask. I guess I lost my temper a little bit."

Actually, the punter had poked at Sayers, and the two exchanged harsh words. Later, both cooled off, knowing quite well that pro football is not a gentle game.

One way to figure out the value of Gale Sayers in his rookie year is to resort to statistics. For example, although Chicago lost its first three ball games, once Gale became the regular starting running back, they scored nine victories in their next 11 games. On an individual basis, Gale had handled the ball a total of 232 times, including rushing, pass receiving, kickoffs and punt returns. He had gained 2,272 yards, which averaged out to 9.8 yards every time he got his hands on the football. He had scored 22 touchdowns, which established a new N.F.L. record; and had scored 132 points, a new record for rookies.

Before Sayers' magnificent effort against San Francisco, he and Bob Hayes of the Dallas Cowboys had been running neck and neck for Rookie-of-the-Year honors. After the game was over, there was no contest—Gale Sayers was the undisputed winner.

Gale knew he had been lucky. As he said after the season, "I never expected to do this well in the pros." He had probably expected to be injured during a ball game, for that was common in the professional ranks. He still had to prove that he could get up and walk back to the huddle after the huge defensive ends and tackles banged into him solidly. And he knew that he would be a special target the next year.

Already the defensive coaches of other teams were starting to figure out his style of running. Wayne Walker, who had played a great defensive game for the Detroit Lions that year, pointed out that most other running backs were leaning forward when they drove into the line. In fact, they were leaning forward so far that, once they did break through, they practically fell down by themselves. But not Gale Sayers. He leaned forward, too, but when he did have the opportunity to slip through the line, he could regain his balance in a fraction of a second and be running in an erect position. "He's the greatest offensive threat I've ever played against," said Walker during the following season. "This year he's running harder than last year."

During the 1967 season, Sayers found that opposing players were dogging his footsteps no matter where he went. For rival coaches had learned that stopping Sayers meant stopping the Chicago Bears, and they instructed their defenses to go all-out.

But nobody could stop the great ball-carrier for long. Late in the season, he victimized the San Francisco 49ers, just as he had done in his rookie year. This time he scored three touch-

Sayers outdistances Kermit Alexander of the 49ers.

In the last half of the Falcons' game Sayers is stopped cold by Tommy Nobis.

downs. He opened the game by grabbing the kickoff on his three-yard line and bolting 97 yards through the mud and rain for the score. Next, he took a pitchout on his 15-yard line and sloshed through for touchdown number-two. Finally, he plucked a punt out of the air on his 42, and scooted 58 yards for the third six-pointer.

The following week, against the Vikings, he picked up 131 yards in 20 carries. In one play he ran 38 yards to set up a Chicago field goal, which put the Bears ahead, 3-0. After that, the Vikings went ahead, and it seemed that Sayers would pose no further threats while the Minnesotans remained zeroed in on him. But then Chicago's Lionel Taylor intercepted a pass to give his team possession on the Viking 39. A pass to Johnny Morris brought the ball down to the 21. And then Sayers, with runs of 17 and seven yards, scored two touchdowns to put the Bears in the lead again. But in spite of Gale's efforts the game ended in a 10-10 tie.

Against Atlanta, in the season's final game, Gale ran for 104 yards in 11 carries. The last half yielded only 20 of those yards because the Falcons had set their sights on number 40 and had halted him. However, by then the Kansas Comet had scored two touchdowns. For the first, Gale raced 51 yards in spectacular fashion through the entire enemy defense. Four times it seemed that he would be stopped, but somehow he managed to keep his feet moving as he broke the tackles and surged ahead over the final chalk mark. The other touchdown was scored on a 32-yard pass play.

Gale finished third in the 1967 rushing statistics. The winner was Leroy Kelly of Cleveland, who had amassed 1,205 yards in 235 carries for a 5.1 average. Sayers had carried the ball 186 times (from scrimmage) and gained 880 yards for a 4.7 average.

Yet those figures did not really tell the full story of his running power. In the San Francisco game, for example, his 97-yard kickoff return and 58-yard punt runback did not count in figuring out the rushing statistics. But they amounted to 155 yards worth of running.

Statistics seldom tell the full story of a ball player. They cannot really measure Gale Sayers' inspirational value to the team. As long as he is in the line-up, the Bears know they have the breakaway runner who is capable of turning a ball game around with one or two long dashes. He is their big gun, the man who can make them a winning team.

And Gale is a man they can be proud of, a fine,

warm, sensitive human being. He doesn't talk much, but when he does it comes from his heart. He is no longer able to use his position as a football star to make headlines in sit-in demonstrations; and the job he does as a public-spirited citizen does not always reach the newspapers. Yet, in his way, he contributes a great deal.

For example, once a crowd of almost 1,000 boys packed into Chicago's Wendell Phillip High School to hear him speak, and he told them a strange story:

"A man I know, who was born in a sod hut, could have been a lawyer. He had an uncle who offered to send him through college and on to law school. But the man dropped out of high school when he was in the tenth grade. So, instead of becoming a lawyer and wearing nice clothes and sitting in a clean office, he now works as a car washer in a used-car lot."

The boys started to laugh, and Sayers waited until they were through. When the laughter subsided he continued with a sad sort of smile on his lips.

"The man I'm talking about is my father. He works long hours and comes home at night very tired from his day's work. He earns seventy-five dollars a week. Off and on he's been doing that for more than thirty-five years."

Most of the kids got the message. The difference between being a professional man with a good job and being a car washer with low pay lay in getting a good education.

Behind expert blocking, Gale carries the ball through Packer defenses.

Gale Sayers is a quiet sort of person. But he feels that if he can save just one kid from being a school dropout every time he talks, he would be willing to make a speech each day in the year.

THE TEST
OF A ROOKIE
JIM HART

There was an encouraging smile on the face of St. Louis coach Charley Winner as he pointed his finger at young Jim Hart.

"You're my quarterback this season, son," he said. "I'm going to stick with you all the way."

For Hart this was a dream come true. But Coach Winner had great misgivings. He knew that he was putting the young man on the spot. Hart was green, untested. His total pro football experience consisted of eight minutes of action during the final game of the 1966 season. Nobody was sure this rookie could guide a big-league team through 14 rugged games.

Yet there was nothing else that could be done. Only a few days previously, the Cardinals had received word that Charley Johnson, their outstanding regular quarterback, had been called up for Army duty. Johnson, who was an officer in the reserves, had known that he might have to report at any time, but he had thought the Army might not want him because of a recent operation to correct a knee injury. But the Army had examined him, found him fit and ordered him into uniform.

Johnson was the man St. Louis counted on to lead the team to victory in the 1967 season. He had proved himself one of the outstanding passers in the league. Steady, cool under pressure, possessing a good arm and the instinctive ability to call the right play at the right time, Johnson was the kind of quarterback every team wanted. He was a born leader.

Of course, Johnson had once been a rookie, too. When he came to the Cardinals back in 1961, he had done very little in the way of leading. The records show that he had thrown only 13 passes and completed just five for a total of 51 yards. The Cardinals, however, realized how good he was, and he soon proved that they were not mistaken in their judgment. By the fourth game of the following season he had become their regular quarterback.

The rest of the N.F.L. also realized Johnson's importance to the Cardinals and they always tried to zero in on him. They knew that when he was out of the St. Louis line-up, the team was in trouble. The Cardinals' record during the 1965 and 1966 seasons proved that. During those two seasons St. Louis had played a total of 28 games. While Johnson was unhurt and calling the signals, the Cards won 11, lost two and tied one. But while he was injured and couldn't play, the "Big Red," as the team was known, won only two games and lost 12. The statistics told the whole story in this case. The Cards were a threat to the rest of the league only while Johnson was on the field. Without him they were just doormats for the other teams.

But St. Louis realized there was no use crying about the situation. The welfare of the country was obviously much more important than a game of football. The Cardinals would have to seek the best solution to their problem as possible. So, before settling on Jim Hart, they tried desperately to get another quarterback who had some experience.

They asked about the availability of such players as Gary Cuozzo of the New Orleans Saints, Earl Morrall of the Giants and Norm Snead of the Eagles. They also tried to obtain Bill Munson and Jim Ninowski. But they were turned down in each instance. The Chicago Bears said that Jack Concannon was available, but they demanded too high a price for him. St. Louis also had an opportunity to get George Mira, the substitute quarterback of the San Francisco 49ers. But Mira had not played very much and was as big a risk as any of the other rookies the Cardinals had in training camp.

St. Louis had just four possible choices. One was Charley Johnson, who would probably receive special passes enabling him to join the team over the weekends. However, weekends weren't good enough. To be effective, a quarterback has to practice with the team constantly. He has to be available for strategy sessions with his coaches to plot out new plays and watch movies that show how enemy defenses operate. Although Johnson was welcome to attend the St. Louis games and get into a football uniform to be ready for emergency duty, he could not serve as the regular quarterback.

The other three choices were Jim Hart, rookie Tim Van Galder of Iowa State, and another rookie, Vidal Carlin of North Texas State. One of these three would have to take over as regular quarterback, and it looked as if Jim Hart was the man.

When the Cardinals announced their decision to rely on the rookie, sportswriters went scurrying to the record books. They wanted to find out how many other rookies had become regulars at the quarterback position and how well they had done. What they learned showed that young Jim Hart would be under unusual pressure.

Yes, it had been done before, but the results were far from encouraging. Randy Johnson had taken over with the Atlanta Falcons, and Fran Tarkenton with the Minnesota Vikings. But those men were playing for teams which had just been organized as part of the National Football League's expansion program. Not only was it the first year for the quarterbacks, but for the teams as well. And neither team had ended up with a winning record.

Even an established club had tried a rookie quarterback, but with unfortunate results. The Washington Redskins had used Norm Snead and the season had ended in disaster. The Redskins had won one, lost 12 and tied one.

Only one quarterback had ever succeeded as a rookie. That was the great Bob Waterfield, who

During a practice session Hart fires a pass while Coach
Winner directs the receivers.

had played with the Cleveland Browns in the days when the Browns were part of the old All-America Conference. However, that league hadn't been nearly as tough as the N.F.L.

All pro football coaches, including Charley Winner, agreed that it took several years before a quarterback knew enough about the position to take over. Such outstanding players as Bart Starr of the Packers, Frank Ryan of the Browns and Sonny Jurgenson (who had been with the Eagles in his rookie days) of the Redskins all spent three years sitting on the bench, watching the first-string signal callers in action, before they became starters themselves.

There were so many things a quarterback had to learn. He had to know where the other teams were weakest so that he could direct his attention to those spots. He had to be able to "read" the enemy's defenses so that he would know instantly what they were going to do to stop his plays. Then, to outwit them, he could change the play at the line of scrimmage by calling an audible.

These were only a few of the problems a quarterback had to face. Learning how to adjust to difficult situations as they arose took time and experience. And Jim Hart had very little experience playing pro football. In fact, only a year before, the Cardinals did not believe he was even big league material. Neither did any other pro team. He had never done anything to make them think he could make the grade.

Jim Hart had been a pretty good football player at Niles West High School in Niles, Illinois. He had received scholarship offers from such universities as Indiana, Wisconsin, Northwestern, Miami and Arizona. However, he had chosen to attend Southern Illinois University, a medium-sized school located in Carbondale, Illinois. He chose S.I.U. over the others because he honestly thought he would have trouble keeping up his marks if he attended a large college.

Jim had always belittled himself in one way or another. When he was just a youngster, he considered entering a "punt-pass-and-place-kick" competition which was to be held in nearby Evanston, but he hesitated because he thought he didn't have a chance. His stepfather, Fred Gilbert, encouraged him to go ahead and try anyway. The boy entered the contest and, to his surprise, he won.

Playing for Southern Illinois proved to be a disheartening experience for Jim. Most of the time the team ended up on the short end of the score. Once, during his sophomore year, S.I.U. managed to upset Northern Michigan by a score of 27-0, but only because Hart passed for three touchdowns and scored the other himself. During his last two years the club won just four out of 20 games.

However, those losses weren't Jim's fault. As his coach, Don Shroyer, said later, "Most of the time he was trying to throw the ball while he was on the seat of his pants."

In 1966, his senior year, Jim was the only regular with any college experience. The other 10 were sophomores. Many times Hart would drop back to pass and find himself surrounded by the other team. And when he did manage to get loose long enough to throw, his receivers would often drop the ball.

Yet, in spite of his poor pass-completion record, Jim fully expected to join a pro team. He had been contacted by the Los Angeles Rams, who told him not to worry because they would be in touch with him soon. Hart waited for the Rams to call, but they never did.

Still there was a good chance that he would be chosen in the 1966 draft of college players. Surely there was a team that could use a quarterback who had a strong arm, was well built and able to take a lot of punishment.

But Jim waited in vain. No team in the National

or American Football Leagues wanted him. He watched them pick such unknowns as Jim LeClair of C. W. Post College, Dave Neilson of Albion and Ron Meyer of South Dakota State.

Ironically, his college coach was the person who gave him the opportunity to play pro football. Don Shroyer had left Southern Illinois to take a position as assistant coach with the Cardinals. When the college draft was over, he told Head Coach Winner about the 6-foot 2-inch quarterback. Since the Cards had nothing to lose, they invited Hart to their training camp to show his skills.

Hart tried out. The Cards liked what they saw and made him an offer. When Hart signed his contract he wasn't thinking about money. He was a member of the St. Louis Cardinal football team, and that was what counted. Later, he jokingly commented that he had received the smallest bonus in the history of the National Football League.

Jim was the number-three quarterback, behind Charley Johnson and Terry Nofsinger. As a member of the taxi squad, he had the job of keeping records of the Cardinal's offensive plays and the defenses used by the other teams.

As he watched Johnson work Jim realized that he had a lot to learn about quarterbacking. He marveled at the way Johnson was able to read the enemy's defenses and call for just the right play at the right time. With "good old Charley" calling the signals the Cards were continually fighting for the top spot in their division.

And then, for the second time in two years, Johnson was injured. When he was forced out of the line-up, there were still five games left on the 1966 schedule, and the Cards were making a strong bid for the Division title. After substitute quarterback Terry Nofsinger took over for Johnson, St. Louis' hopes promptly went down the drain. Nofsinger was unable to move the team, and by the end of the season the Cardinals were in fourth place.

Hart thought that he would get his chance to play at that time. Nofsinger had failed to establish his right to the job and Hart thought that he certainly couldn't do much worse. But Coach Winner only promoted Jim to the field telephone, from which he relayed spotters' information.

By the time Hart stepped out on a football field, the 1966 season had eight minutes to go. The Cards were playing the Cleveland Browns, and were behind by 30 points. Winner tapped Jim on the shoulder and sent him into the game with only one set of instructions: he was to throw the ball as often as possible.

Jim complied. On the very first play he dropped far back and shot a screen pass to Willis Crenshaw. The pass was completed—for a loss of two yards!

In all, Jim Hart was in the ball game for a total of 17 plays. He attempted 11 passes and completed only four of them. Three of his throws were right on target, but the receivers dropped the ball.

From the Cards' point of view, Hart had done nothing to earn a promotion. But they also knew that Nofsinger wasn't their man. So they traded Nofsinger, confident that they could pick up an experienced passer to act as a backup man for Charley Johnson before the 1967 season got under way.

But they didn't. And when Johnson was called into the Army, there was nobody available except two rookies and the man they had not thought enough of to draft in 1966, Jim Hart.

For all practical purposes, Hart was a rookie, too. A total of 17 plays in a game that was already lost hardly qualified him as an experienced signal-caller. He had never started in a pro game, never had the pressure on him and had never been in a really tough situation. He was as green as the other rookies.

Hart was finally chosen simply because quarterback coach Harry Gilmer thought he had the best arm in camp and knew enough to get rid of the ball quickly. This last ability was extremely important, and the lack of it had been one of Terry Nofsinger's problems. He had not yet perfected a "quick release."

The first game on the Cardinals' exhibition schedule was against the newest team in the league, the New Orleans Saints. Coach Winner planned to use Hart for the first half, then give his other two newcomers one period each. The Saints made sure that Winner stuck to his plan, for on the final play of the first half Jim Hart was hit so hard that he had to be helped off the field. He wasn't seriously hurt—he just had the wind knocked out of him—but Coach Winner gave him the rest of the day off anyway.

Although Jim had spent only two short periods on the field, during that time he had demonstrated a surprising amount of ability. He had tried 18 passes and had completed 14 of them, good for a total of 198 yards. Of the four passes that missed connections, one was dropped and another intercepted. One of his special targets was rookie receiver Dave Williams, a man with great legs and the ability to outleap almost anybody in the pros. Hart hit Williams four times, once with a 47-yard beauty. Hart also threw a

19-yard pass to flanker Billy Gambrell, who went for a touchdown.

However, not everything the rookie did was right. His most glaring mistake occurred when the Cards had the ball with a third down coming up and only a few inches to go for the first down. The New Orleans line bunched up shoulder to shoulder, ready to meet the plunge. An experienced quarterback would have realized that he had a wide-open area behind the defensive line and would have changed the play at the line of scrimmage. Hart didn't call an audible, however. Instead he handed off to Willis Crenshaw, who was stacked up and failed to get the first down. The Cards lost to the Saints by a 23-14 score.

The following week they lost to Pittsburgh, too. But in spite of the losses, Hart showed that he could remain cool under fire and could throw the kind of passes that hurt the other team. During the game with Pittsburgh he threw a 26-yarder to Dave Williams, who ran to the Steeler one-yard line before being knocked down.

One of Jim's greatest attributes was his refusal to give anything less than his best effort, no matter what the score was. He demonstrated his determination while playing against the Bears. Before the end of the first half it became obvious that the Cards were getting slaughtered. In good

During the preseason exhibition game against Chicago, Hart throws over the outstretched arms of defender Doug Buffone.

part it was Jim's own fault, for three of his passes had been intercepted and Chicago had turned all three into touchdowns. Yet the young quarterback kept plugging way. The Bears were ahead by 35-0 before Hart threw a touchdown pass to backfield ace Johnny Roland. When Roland scored there were only four seconds left in the first half. Hart also threw a touchdown pass to Sonny Randle in the fourth period. After that, however, the Cards were unable to add any more points. The final score was 42-14.

St. Louis won only one exhibition game, and that was against the Baltimore Colts. Neither

In the Cardinals' only preseason victory, Hart (17) watches as Prentice Gautt breaks through the center of the Colt line.

team was able to produce a touchdown, and the final score was 9-5. Hart consoled himself with the fact that the great Johnny Unitas couldn't throw a touchdown pass, either.

But the Baltimore and St. Louis coaches were all impressed with the rookie's showing. As the game movies showed later, seven of Hart's passes could have been caught, and three of them would have been touchdowns. On one attempt he threw a long pass toward Billy Gambrell, who was a step ahead of the defense man guarding him. But the defender screened the ball from the flanker's sight. As Gambrell reached up blindly, the pass went right through his hands and fell harmlessly to the ground. Hart's pass proved that he could not only throw for distance, but that he had a great deal of accuracy as well.

Jim also showed that he could take care of himself when he was in trouble. Late in the second quarter he dropped back to pass and found that Bubba Smith, the huge All-America rookie tackle from Michigan State, was driving in on him. Smith dove and managed to grab Hart's foot. Hart shook free, turned and hit Gambrell with a comeback pass.

The 23-year-old rookie was starting to learn the art of playing the quarterback position. He discovered how to throw the ball out of bounds

Hart hits Billy Gambrell with a pass.

when his receivers were covered, and yet not make it appear as if he was intentionally grounding the ball, which would have meant a penalty for his team. To take advantage of his teammates' blocking, he always tried to stay "in the pocket" as much as possible. He had learned the importance of this tactic from Don Shroyer when the latter was coaching him at Southern Illinois. Most college quarterbacks like to roll out, but Shroyer had warned Hart that the pros would knock him right into the grandstand if he tried it too often against them.

In spite of their poor exhibition record, the Cardinals were favored to win the regular-season opener against the injury-riddled New York Giants. Half-a-dozen men whom the Giants had counted on to bolster their defense had been hurt. Some were out of the line-up for the whole year, and the season had not yet begun. But, as it turned out, the Giants walloped the Cards by a score of 37-20.

The game was a nightmare for young Jim Hart. Earlier he had been so nervous that he could hardly eat a thing. The fact that he was playing before hometown fans unsettled him even more. They would be watching him, a raw rookie who was trying to take over for their idol, Charley Johnson.

Hart became even more upset after the Giants intercepted four of his passes. Three of the interceptions took place in the last half, and on all three occasions the Giants drove over for a touchdown. The disappointed fans, impatient with the rookie, began to boo him. They chose to overlook the fact that Hart had completed 10 of his 24 attempts for an impressive total of 153 yards. Although they didn't know it at the time, that same day Bart Starr of the Packers also saw four of his passes intercepted by the Detroit Lions' defense. Yet nobody booed Starr.

Jim was disgusted with himself. He felt that he had let the Cardinals down. As he said later, "I played a rotten game. I felt like a dumb kid out there, throwing away the ball game."

But, when the players got together for their post-game dinner, all of them came over to speak to Hart. One by one they patted him on the back and told him he had done his best. The words each player added were almost the same: "Forget it, kid. We're going to win. We start next week."

In their next game the Cardinals were underdogs against Pittsburgh. Nobody gave St. Louis much of a chance as long as the rookie kept throwing the ball where the enemy could reach it. But the Steelers intercepted only one of Hart's passes that day. In addition, his passing gained

Hart runs for a touchdown against the Steelers.

137 yards, even though he completed just eight out of 23 tries. Jim Bakken, the fine St. Louis place kicker, booted seven field goals to set a new record, and Hart ran 23 yards to score a touchdown. It wasn't a particularly good effort by Hart, but the Cards won, and that was what counted.

In spite of the victory, St. Louis wasn't expected to do very well against the powerful Detroit Lions, who had won one game and had tied the mighty Green Bay Packers. Later, some of the Cardinals said that this contest was the turning point in Jim Hart's career as a pro quarterback.

At one point the Lions were ahead by a score of 7-0, and the Cardinals had the ball deep in their own territory. Hoping to cross up the opposition, Hart called for a pass. With the snap of the ball from center, the Lions surged in like a tidal wave, and Hart retreated into his own end zone. He stopped, turned and threw. But Detroit's Darris McCord, after blitzing in, got his hand on the ball and tipped it to teammate Larry Hand, who bulled ahead for a touchdown and ran right over Hart in the process.

Hart later said that he had forgotten about the unfortunate play by the time he reached the St. Louis bench. But Cardinal ball carrier Prentice Gautt didn't think so. He said, "The next time we

Detroit's Larry Hand (74) reaches for Hart's unlucky pass, which has been deflected by Darris McCord (78).

went into the huddle, Jim looked five years older!"

Trailing, 14-0, Hart went to work with a vengeance. The Cards scored two quick touchdowns and went on to win, 38-28. The rookie sharpshooter had thrown 19 complete passes in 27 tries for a total of 313 yards. Two of the touchdowns resulted from long bombs that brought the fans to their feet screaming. He threw one to Jackie Smith that covered 57 yards, and another for 48 yards to Billy Gambrell.

The game against the Lions proved that Hart could keep a drive going once it got started. During the five drives that resulted in touchdowns, the young quarterback made good on 15 of 18 pass attempts.

Then St. Louis took on the Minnesota Vikings. Going into the fourth quarter, the Cards were trailing by 11 points. Their only hope was to pass. But as Hart dropped back to allow his receiver to get into position, he slipped and fell down. With the Vikings closing in on him, he got up, rolled out to his left and threw a 40-yard bull's-eye pass to Dave Williams, who went into the end zone for a touchdown. The Cards were back in the game. In that final period Hart completed seven out of 10 clutch passes to lead St. Louis to a 34-24 victory. Once again the rookie had shown what he could do when the chips were down.

When the standings of the clubs were posted the Cardinals, with a record of three straight victories and one defeat, were in first place in the Century Division of the Eastern Conference. And to top it off, rookie Hart, who had been booed for his poor showing in the season's opener, had already been named National Football League offensive player of the week (and he was to win that honor again before the season was over).

Sportswriters began to sit up and take notice. Who was this newcomer? What kind of a man was he? And how did his teammates feel about the kid who had taken Charley Johnson's place?

Football fans found out that Jim Hart was a typical young American who liked to play football and was good at his job. Off the field he was a quiet young man. When he reported for daily practice he carried a brown paper bag containing the lunch packed by his wife.

But once Jim put on a football uniform and walked out on the field, his shyness was gone. He was the Cardinal quarterback and the boss of the team. In his own quiet way, he let the rest of the players know that as long as he was calling the signals he was in charge.

All pro football players know that is how it has to be. They can offer suggestions in the huddle.

The Cardinals accepted Hart as their leader. Here he rallies teammates Jackie Smith (81), Dave Williams (80) and John Roland (23).

Every good quarterback welcomes them because he can't see everything that's going on. But, once the quarterback makes a decision, that is the end of the matter. Only the coach has the right to tell him which play to call.

The players accepted Jim as their leader. And they kidded him about it, too. Once, against the Philadelphia Eagles, the defense crashed through and tackled him hard.

"You know, that really hurt," he said in the huddle.

Tackle Bob Reynolds replied with a twinkle in his eye, "Hey, baby, you're not supposed to take ten seconds to get rid of the ball."

Hart talks with Charley Johnson on the sidelines.

But nobody roughed up Jim Hart very much, for his teammates made every effort to protect the rookie. In the first six games opponents caught him behind the line only twice. During one game, when he came back to the bench with three minutes left to play, a fan sitting in the stands nearby shouted out, "Hey, Hart, your uniform isn't even dirty!"

Jim looked himself over, turned back to the fan and nodded proudly. It was true. Nobody had knocked him down all day.

In spite of his success up to that point, Jim knew that he had had plenty of help. Charley Johnson, who was with the Cardinals on weekends, gave him valuable tips, telling him what he could expect from each team. Often, out of the corner of his eye, Jim would watch Johnson as he stood on the sidelines. He knew how much the regular quarterback wanted to play, yet Johnson was helping him so much that Hart might take away the starting job forever.

Rookie Dave Williams was also helpful, especially as a pass receiver. After the disaster against the New York Giants, Williams told Hart that he was throwing the ball too low. He suggested that Jim get the ball up high so that his receiver could run under it. The tip paid off. Against the Green Bay Packers, one of the outstanding defensive teams in pro football, Williams twice outleaped and outwrestled Herb Adderley to score touchdowns.

Hart's most outstanding weakness was the fact that his passes were often intercepted. Without attempting to make excuses for him, his coaches pointed out that the Cardinals were usually behind in the scoring and had to come from behind to win. The only way to score points in a hurry was to pass. The other teams realized that, too, and were waiting for Hart to throw.

Although St. Louis lost their fifth game to Cleveland, Hart almost managed to pull it out of the fire. Late in the game he engineered a drive that brought St. Louis to the Cleveland 14-yard line. On third down Williams broke free momentarily, but Hart's pass up the middle was knocked down by the alert Cleveland defense.

With their three-game winning streak broken, the Cards went right back to work. This time their opponents were the Philadelphia Eagles. Late in the second quarter of the game, Hart led the Cardinals toward the Philadelphia goal on a sustained drive. He was wisely running out the clock, so that he would score without allowing very much time for the Eagles to retaliate.

Finally, he saw Dave Williams in the end zone and threw a bullet pass to him. Williams leaped up and caught the ball. One official raised his arms in the touchdown signal, but two others ruled that Williams had been out of bounds when his feet touched the ground after his leap. As a result, the score didn't count.

Another quarterback might have been discouraged. But not Hart. Back in the huddle he called for the same play, but it was to go to the other side this time. As Williams broke away, Hart dropped back. The Eagles tore in at him and got through his protective blocking and forced him out of the pocket. He maneuvered to his left, saw his receiver in the clear and put the football right into his hands. This time there wasn't any doubt

Protected from Eagle tacklers by alert blockers, Hart has plenty of time to pass.

in the officials' minds that it was a touchdown.

Hart's cool handling of the situation indicated that he was gradually maturing as a quarterback. Another example of his improvement was his ability to read the Philadelphia defenses.

One of the Eagles' pet defensive plays was the safety blitz. In this play the safetyman, instead of playing back to cover a receiver, would rush into the offensive backfield, trying to reach the quarterback. This gave the defense an extra man for the pass rush. Quite often it turned out to be an effective play.

As he bent over the center, Jim saw telltale signs that the safety blitz was coming. He promptly called an audible. As the Eagles' safety-man raced in, Jackie Smith slipped into the area he had left unprotected. Jim tossed him the ball, and Smith scampered 74 yards for a touchdown. The young quarterback did the same thing again later, using Bobby Joe Conrad this time, and the play resulted in a 31-yard score. The Eagles quickly forgot about safety-blitzing the rookie for the rest of the afternoon. The game ended in a rout and the final score was 48-14.

After that, St. Louis coach Winner began to trust Hart's judgment a great deal more. As the season wore on, he realized he had chosen the right man to take over for Johnson. His new confidence in Hart became apparent in the game against Washington. Prior to that, whenever the Cards were inside the enemy's 10-yard line, the coach had always sent in the play. Against the Redskins, however, Winner left the choice up to Hart. The quarterback called for a tricky look-in pass over the middle of the line to Conrad, and it resulted in a touchdown.

Another milestone in Hart's career was the game which the Cardinals lost to Green Bay. It

Hart looks downfield for a receiver during the game with the Redskins in which he made all the decisions for the first time.

established Jim Hart as a courageous signal caller and a constant threat to throw the long bomb.

At one point during the game, St. Louis was deep in Packer territory. It was fourth down and short yardage to go. Instead of trying for a field goal, Hart decided to attempt the first down. As he bent over the center, he found himself almost face to face with Green Bay's All-Pro middle linebacker, Ray Nitschke, who was "stunting" back and forth; that is, he was moving in and out of the line, yelling at Hart and daring him to run a play through his territory. But Hart kept his head. He ran a ground play away from Nitschke, and the runner made the first down.

During that game Hart bedeviled the opposition with passes that bit off large chunks of yardage. He threw one for 39 yards to Gambrell and one to Jackie Smith for 33 yards; he also threw touchdown passes to Dave Williams, one for 48 yards, the other for 40.

Hart amassed 317 yards passing against the Packers, and very few quarterbacks could boast such a total against them. He kept the Cardinals in the ball game until rookie Travis Williams broke it open by running back a punt 93 yards for a Packer TD. The final score was 31-23.

Most important of all, Hart had begun to come

through with the all-important "third-down play." In pro football, Hart learned, the test of a quarterback is his ability to obtain a first down in such a difficult situation as a third down with five or six yards to go. The defenses know that an ordinary line plunge probably won't make it and that a long pass is too risky. They usually line up expecting a short pass, an end sweep or a draw play. Good quarterbacks, like Johnny Unitas, Bart Starr, Don Meredith and Sonny Jurgenson, usually pick the right play at the right time.

In his winning effort against the Philadelphia Eagles, Hart clicked on eight out of 14 third-down plays, and those eight resulted in 160 valuable yards. His rival, Norm Snead, was not having a particularly good day and could make good on only three of 12 third-down plays. That was one of the reasons for the Eagles' loss.

In spite of his impressive performances, Jim Hart could not seem to conquer his interception jinx. The Chicago Bears intercepted five passes in one game, and that proved costly. By the end of the season 30 of his passes had been picked off by enemy defenses.

This failing contributed to Hart's inability to lead the Cardinals to victory in his rookie year. In fact, the team fell under the .500 mark on the final day of the season, when the Giants beat

Here, Hart has decided to avoid Nitschke (66) and makes

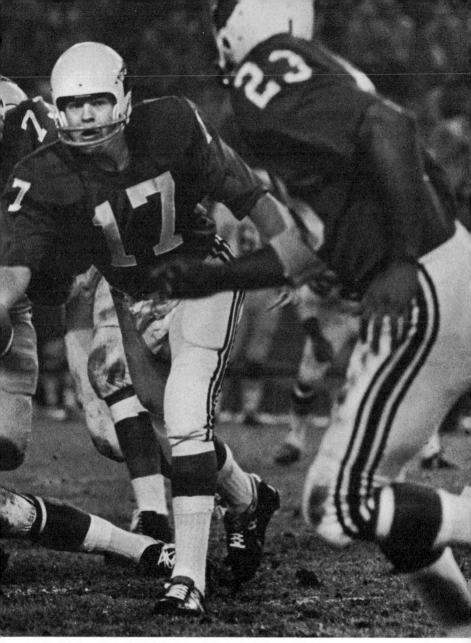

a pitchout to John Roland, who is running to the left.

them again. It wasn't Hart's fault completely. The Cards had suffered a series of damaging injuries. Against the Giants, they had had to play without the services of their best running back, Johnny Roland.

Even so, the Cards threw a scare into New York. Trailing by a score of 7-0, Hart sparked a drive that carried his club down to the Giants' two-yard line just as the first period ended. Then, on the first play of the second quarter, with a tied ball game in sight, Roy Shivers fumbled and New York recovered. That play decided the ball game.

St. Louis finished the season with a record of six victories, seven losses and one tie. Few people had thought they would do so well with a rookie quarterback guiding the team.

Overall, Jim Hart had done well. He showed that he could lead the club and rally them to come from behind. Opposing defenses respected his ability to throw any reasonable distance, and they knew that his throws would be accurate.

The kid nobody wanted had come a long way. Some sportswriters began to compare him with Johnny Unitas. When he had signed with the Colts, the Baltimore all-time great had also been a free agent. Hart was the first one to deny that he was as good as Unitas, though. "I've still got an awful lot to learn," he sighed after the season was over.

Coach Charley Winner's comment about his rookie is perhaps the most perceptive of all: "Jim Hart may never be another Johnny Unitas. But neither will any other quarterback I've seen. The Cardinals will be very happy if Jim Hart lives up to his potential. He can be a real good quarterback."

One thing is certain. If Jim Hart can continue to improve as he did in his rookie season, Charley Johnson might have a fight on his hands when he tries to take back his job as starting quarterback of the St. Louis Cardinals.

THE DOUBTS
OF A ROOKIE
BUBBA SMITH

The huge Michigan State defensive end called
time out, turned and faced the Notre Dame team.
The expression on his face could only be described as part grin and part snarl. The Fighting
Irish bent over in the huddle, trying not to hear
the taunts and sneers of the Spartans' lineman,
but they knew what he was saying. How come the
great Notre Dame team was willing to settle for
a tie? Were they afraid to gamble? This game
was supposed to settle the mythical National

Championship. A tie wouldn't settle anything. Come on, Notre Dame. Stop freezing the ball.

Michigan State fans, warming to the occasion, roared at the sight of their All-America end teasing the mighty Notre Dame squad. Once again they shouted their favorite words at him: "KILL, BUBBA, KILL!"

However, in spite of the goading, undefeated Notre Dame was not going to risk its record by attempting a desperation play against the defenses of undefeated Michigan State. The Irish ran some ground plays, the gun went off and the game ended in a 10-10 tie.

There were people in the stands who were not merely football fans. They were scouts from pro football teams, and they had come because both clubs were loaded with such promising players as defensive lineman Alan Page of Notre Dame, running back Clint Jones of M.S.U.—and the man who had taunted the Notre Dame team, Charles "Bubba" Smith, State's outstanding defensive end.

Watching Smith play and noting his moves on the field, the scouts agreed that Bubba Smith was indeed a magnificent prospect. Standing 6 feet 7 inches tall, weighing about 285 pounds, he seemed capable of knocking down a brick wall.

There were 445 college players scheduled to

Bubba Smith (95) tackles the Notre Dame quarterback.

be drafted by the pros in 1967. Nobody doubted that some ball club would choose Bubba Smith as its first-round draft choice. It would be impossible to ignore a player who had been chosen for the Texas all-state high-school football team and who had been named to the All-America college team two years in succession.

The Baltimore Colts were especially interested in securing Bubba's services. But they had finished in second place in the N.F.L.'s Western Division. As a result, they had to wait for a number of other teams to make their choices before they had a chance. The first choice belonged to the National Football League's newest expansion club, the New Orleans Saints. The only way Baltimore could get a crack at Smith was through a trade with the New Orleans team.

Fortunately, the Saints were willing, and they had no trouble deciding which player they wanted in exchange for the rights to Smith. All pro teams, whether new or old, need a first-class quarterback if they are to succeed. The Colts had two such players in Johnny Unitas and Gary Cuozzo. The latter was often called "the best backup quarterback in the N.F.L." Of course, trading Unitas was out of the question. Baltimore wouldn't part with its All-Pro passer for the entire All-America team. But they were willing to trade Cuozzo.

Nobody thought much about it at the time, but after Bubba joined the team, the Colts' preseason roster included an unusual number of people named Smith. There was Bubba Smith; there was Billy Ray Smith, another Colt defensive tackle, who ironically would be fighting for his job against Bubba. And there was also a man with a very similar name, Willie Ray Smith, Jr., who was scheduled to try out with Baltimore as a running back. Willie Ray, Jr., was Bubba's brother.

In fact, everybody in Bubba's family was in football some way or another. Bubba's father, Willie Ray Smith, Sr., is worthy of a story all by himself. Over a period of more than 20 years, he had compiled one of the most outstanding records ever achieved by any high-school football coach in Texas history. Yet Coach Smith had never played college football. In 1942, when he was out of a job and looking for almost any kind of work, he had heard that a junior high school in Orange, Texas, was looking for a football coach. Mr. Smith had bought a few books about football and read them. Then he attended some seminars on football at various coaching clinics. Somehow he got the job.

At first even the youngsters he was trying to coach knew more about football than he did. But he learned and went on to become tops in his field.

Bubba grew up in a house that was always full of football players because his mother looked after them. Coach Smith insisted that his players eat full meals after practice, but most of them couldn't afford it. So Mrs. Smith fed them with food meant for her own family. Many times Bubba found that his lunch was cut down because part of it had been eaten by somebody his father had brought to the house.

Football was the chief topic of conversation in the Smith household, day or night. Many times Mr. Smith would wake up at 5 o'clock in the morning with the inspiration for a new play. He would rout the boys out of bed, and they would all go downstairs and design the play, drawing diagrams until the elder Smith was satisfied.

Mrs. Smith wasn't left out, either. Once she attended a game played by her husband's team. When the boys started dropping behind in the scoring, she scribbled a note hastily and sent it to the bench, using Bubba as a messenger. The note read, "If you want to start winning this game, stop using the I-formation and get into a Wing-T!"

The elder Smith had little patience with players who did not pay attention or refused to concentrate on what he was saying.

"Dad would tell you how to do a thing once and show it to you," Bubba said of his father. "If you didn't get it, he'd use a blackboard to spell it out for you. If you still didn't get it, he'd climb all over you, questioning your desire and hustle. By the time he got finished, you'd feel so bad about not learning, you'd work yourself to death."

In 1957, Mr. Smith became the head coach at Charlton-Pollard High School in Beaumont, Texas. The Smith family soon made the school famous throughout the state. Mr. Smith coached nine district and three state championship teams, and his three sons, Willie Ray, Jr., Bubba and Larry "Tody" Smith, earned all-state honors. Willie Ray, Jr., went on to attend Kansas University, where he played in the same backfield as Gale Sayers. After college graduation Willie tried out with the Kansas City Chiefs of the American Football League, but failed to make the team because of knee trouble.

A year after his brother Willie Ray started to play for Charlton-Pollard, young Bubba donned a uniform and became the team's regular center. He found that he was up against some rugged opposition. Several of the players he faced— most of whom were his personal friends—went on to join the pros: Mel Farr went to the Detroit Lions, "Earthquake" Hunt to Boston and Ernie Ladd to Kansas City.

In Texas, high-school football games have always attracted large crowds, and Bubba often found himself playing before thousands of people. A game attended by 15,000 or 20,000 fans was nothing out of the ordinary, and when Charlton-Pollard faced its arch rival, Herber High, the contest drew 45,000.

In Bubba's senior year, his team went through the season undefeated, posting a record of 10 wins and no losses. South Park High had a record of nine victories and only one loss. For a while there was a great debate over which team was better. Perhaps, if they had faced each other, the issue would have been decided. But they did not meet, for Charlton-Pollard was a Negro school and South Park was white.

Today, segregation is not as common in sports. White and Negro teams often play against each other. And nobody is happier about integrated football than Coach Smith, who says of the white schools with a smile, "How about those guys! They're trying to steal all my best players!"

Bubba was a big boy when he started playing football, but he seemed to get bigger almost overnight. Most of his growing occurred at the age of 14. That year, in only four-and-a-half months, his height zoomed from 6 feet 1 inch to 6 feet 7 inches, and his weight rose from 202 pounds to 224.

However, there was no blubber on Bubba. As he described himself, he had no fat and no stomach—just a long chest. By the time he was finished growing and was out of college, he wore a size-20 shirt, size-14½ shoes, and his suit jackets were size-54 extra long.

Strangely enough, he had never been a big eater—that is, he never ate a great deal of food at one sitting. However, he did have a meal every three or four hours and downed five glasses of milk each time.

Naturally, Bubba received a host of college offers. After mulling them over, he narrowed the choice to U.C.L.A. and Michigan State. Bubba wanted to go to the California school because his good friend, Mel Farr, had also elected to go there. But Mr. Smith, who was a great friend and admirer of Michigan State's head coach, Duffy Daugherty, whom he had met at a football clinic, advised against the West Coast school. He said that there were too many distracting influences in a big city like Los Angeles and Bubba would not get an education because he would be too busy seeing the sights.

So Charles "Bubba" Smith enrolled as a fresh-man at Michigan State. He still relishes telling the story of his first day at school because it proves how fearsome-looking he was as a boy still in his teens.

Bubba had no idea who his roommate would be when he went to his assigned room, stretched out on a bed and dozed off. A few moments later he heard a sound at the door. Startled, Bubba leaped from the bed, strode across the room and opened it. The boy at the door looked up, saw what he must have thought was an escaped mon-ster and ran for his life. Bubba's roommate turned out to be a mild-mannered, 140-pound premedical student.

There was never any doubt that Bubba would make the Spartans' varsity the moment he was eligible. By his sophomore year he had achieved almost full growth, but had lost none of his blazing speed. In high school he could run the 100-yard dash in 10.3 seconds.

One day, while the M.S.U. squad was taking a break, the subject of speed came up. Bubba challenged the backfield players to a 50-yard dash. Coach Daugherty, who liked to encourage competition among his men, marked off the distance. From an even start, Bubba beat quarterback Steve Juday by five yards. Then he raced fullback Eddie Cotton and won by four yards.

Nor was his fleetness of foot simply the kind that shows up in practice but not in a game. Playing against Penn State, he chased Mike Irwin, the Nittany Lions' fastest back, as he was speeding toward the goal on a kickoff return. He overtook Irwin from behind and knocked him down. Before being stopped, Irwin had outrun the entire Michigan State team.

And, of course, Bubba was a stone wall in the line. He was double-teamed and sometimes even triple-teamed, but nothing seemed to work very well against him. After the Penn State game a

Smith moves in to tackle the ball-carrier, Bill Rettig of Penn State.

newspaper account said: ". . . Smith converted their offense to rubble."

When sportswriters, looking at his huge bulk, once kidded him by saying, "You don't feed Bubba, you just oil him like any other machine," the All-America end responded quietly by saying, "I'm big, but I get tired just like anybody else. I'm human."

Against the powerful Ohio State running attack, Bubba found himself the target of gang-blocking again. In one play the huge defensive end ripped through the interference, brushed aside the final man and banged down the ball carrier for a five-yard loss.

That single play, more than any other, made Ohio State realize the game was lost. It turned out to be a 34-7 disaster for the Buckeyes, and they ended the day with a total of *minus 22 yards rushing,* the worst record in the school's history.

In his junior year Bubba was simply magnificent, but as a senior he didn't seem to do very much. The reason for his comparative lack of success wasn't difficult to find—nobody was running his way. Other teams ran plays to the other side of the line once they saw what Bubba could do. Bubba was unhappy because he felt he needed the practice. For he knew that once he got to the pros nobody would be running away from him. But, as M.S.U. defensive coach Henry "The Bull" Bullough said, "He scared more ball carriers than he tackled."

Watching Bubba crouch and then get off the line quickly, Bullough realized that he had great potential, and the defensive coach wanted to make sure that Bubba lived up to it. So he needled, prodded and pushed him to the limit— and then he pushed him some more.

Bubba both hated and loved his coach. He hated him because Bullough made him work hard every minute he was on the field.

He realized, however, that Bullough would

not have taken the trouble to bear down on him if he had not felt Bubba had skills worth developing. In that way the defensive coach was very much like his own father, demanding only his best efforts, advising and steering him in the right direction. And Bubba loved the coach for being so concerned.

In a way, Bullough's intensive coaching was a drawback. Once Bubba understood what the Spartan coach was saying, the rest came naturally. He made it look so easy that many people thought he was lazy. The crowds, watching his pantherlike body coiled to spring at ball carriers, tried to goad him to further efforts by chanting, "KILL, BUBBA, KILL!"

Bubba hated to leave Michigan State. He had enjoyed the comradeship of the players. And he knew that there would be a gaping hole at his position, which would be difficult to fill. The coaches were just as sad to see him go, but they consoled themselves with the knowledge that Bubba's "baby brother," Tody, would be along soon.

When Bubba returned home after graduation, he found that his younger brother was about as big as he was. In the past Bubba had loved to tease the boy, but now his mother put a stop to such antics.

"Don't fool with Tody," she warned. "He'll break your jaw." Tody proved her point by smacking a wooden door with his fist and cracking it all the way down to its frame. Bubba turned away in mock horror, but with a proud grin on his face. His brother seemed to be quite capable of taking care of himself.

Now that he was out of college, Bubba Smith had good reason to feel confident of his future. Not only had he been chosen for the All-Star squad, which was to play against the champion Green Bay Packers, but he was also the number-one draft choice in the country. At least the Baltimore Colts thought so.

However, sportswriters and pro coaches were quick to point out that being the number-one pick didn't really mean very much. True, many had made good in a big way: Charley Trippi, Tommy Harmon, Kyle Rote and Paul Hornung. But others had never achieved stardom: Terry Baker, King Hill, Harry Gilmer, George Shaw. Some greats, such as Johnny Unitas, had never been picked by anybody. What counted was performance, not college reputation.

Originally, Bubba had been slated to take over the defensive-end position in Baltimore's line-up. The Colts needed a replacement for their great All-Pro end, Gino Marchetti, who had retired.

However, after considering their roster carefully, the coaches decided that the team needed help at the tackle slot. Undoubtedly, Bubba could make the switch with no trouble.

Perhaps Head Coach Don Shula hoped that the rookie would develop in the tradition of another immense tackle, the late Gene "Big Daddy" Lipscomb. He had been a tower of strength in the Baltimore line. Even the great Jimmy Brown had been very careful not to make Lipscomb angry, for there was no telling what he might do to a ball carrier. Lipscomb's simple philosophy of playing the game was, "I just bust in and tackle everybody in sight. Then I sort 'em out and keep the guy who's got the football." Maybe, with Bubba Smith's great strength, size and speed, he would turn out to be the same kind of ball player.

But for a while it seemed that Bubba would not play any position for Baltimore. Willie Ray Smith, Jr., had been promised a chance to make the club's regular-season roster, but the Colts had released him. Bubba was angry. He thought his older brother had not received a fair tryout and that Baltimore had gone back on its word. He demanded to be traded to the Kansas City Chiefs, who also wanted him.

As a matter of fact, for a short time it seemed

that Bubba might not play football at all. The Baltimore Bullets of the National Basketball Association had also offered him a contract. They needed a strong player who could stand under the basket to grab rebounds. They reasoned that, with Bubba's strength, nobody could push him out of the way.

Strangely enough, whatever reputation Bubba had as a basketball player stemmed from his high-school days. He had not played the game at all in college, although he had liked to practice in the gym occasionally.

Bubba's father soon put an end to all that foolishness. Bubba was a football player and had no business thinking about basketball. He cooled him down and made him see how unreasonably he was acting. If Willie Ray couldn't make the team, that was his own hard luck. If he had been good enough, the Colts surely would have signed him. Mr. Smith was able to talk his younger son into reporting to Baltimore after all.

But before Bubba got down to serious summer training, he had to play in the All-Star game against the Packers. He was initiated into the mysteries of professional football in a hurry. On his first play from scrimmage, he was hit by Jerry Kramer and Forrest Gregg, two of the best, most experienced offensive linemen in the league. On the third play he was taken out by a blind-side block delivered by Packer center Ken Bowman. Soon he was knocked off his feet again by Kramer. Gale Gillingham also chipped in with some telling blocks on the rookie.

By that time Bubba had begun to get the idea. Sheer strength wasn't going to be enough; he had to get the jump on Kramer to be effective. Fortunately, Bubba was especially good at beating an offensive guard in getting off the line. Like a shot he was past Kramer, piling into Bart Starr and smacking him down for a 10-yard loss. Later in the game he tackled the quarterback for another loss. He was also able to upset one of Green Bay's pet plays—a power sweep around end. Bubba slipped through the Packers' offensive line and knocked halfback Donny Anderson for a six-yard loss.

But the All-Stars couldn't score against the National League champions, who beat them by a score of 27-0. It was the Packers' second successive shutout against All-Star competition. After the game, Bubba Smith was named the Most Valuable Player on the All-Star squad.

When asked whether Bubba was the best rookie he ever played against, Jerry Kramer said frankly that he wasn't. "A couple of years back I tangled with a guy named Merlin Olsen, who now plays an awful lot of defense for the Los Angeles Rams," Kramer said. "But Bubba can be a good one. No doubt about it."

Kramer and other Packers pointed out that Bubba was guessing too much of the time.

"We ran right at him, and he'd move right or left, depending on which way he thought the runner would go. By doing that he took himself out of the play."

Kramer's criticism made sense. Bubba had tried to outsmart the veteran Green Bay blockers running interference for fullback Jim Grabowski. When the blockers ran right at him, he would try to anticipate the direction in which Grabowski would run to avoid him. For example, when Bubba moved to the right, Grabowski would run to the left. As a result of Bubba's ill-advised maneuvers, the Green Bay fullback gained a good deal of yardage.

In spite of his All-Star experience, Bubba remained as self-assured as ever. "The pros aren't so tough," he said after the game. He shrugged off the fact that he had allowed himself to be trapped out of a play on a number of occasions. Instead, he proudly pointed out how many times the Packers had double-teamed him.

Back at the Colt training camp, Bubba began practice in earnest. One of his first sessions was what Colt coaches call "the Oklahoma drill." It consists of man-to-man competition—an offensive player against a defensive player. Bubba lined up against offensive guard Dale Memelaar. The next thing he knew, Memelaar had brushed him roughly aside and almost knocked him off his feet. Puzzled, Bubba went to the sidelines and watched. He had been practicing with a badly bruised shoulder (which he hadn't told the coaches about) and he had not really understood what he was expected to do. But now he observed the other players and learned from their moves.

Next, he lined up against Danny Sullivan, a 6-foot 3-inch, 250-pound veteran with six years of pro experience. Now Bubba knew what to do. He put both hands on Sullivan's shoulders and shoved hard, then hit him with his right forearm across the neck and shoulders. Down went Sullivan face-first!

"Give him to me again," Sullivan said. He lined up against Bubba. And he was beaten again.

"Once more," said the determined Sullivan. He faced Bubba again. This time he stopped the rookie.

Later Sullivan said, "Bubba is strong and he's quick. A man has to go all-out to beat him."

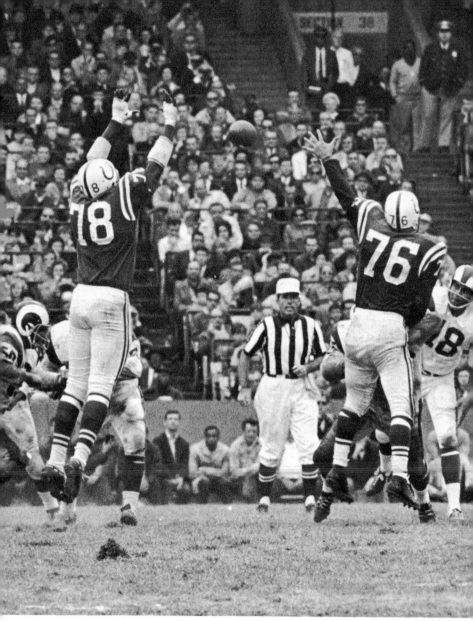

Bubba Smith (78) reaches up to deflect a pass from Ram quarterback Roman Gabriel.

Cocky, slow-talking Bubba Smith fit into the Baltimore squad as if it was a comfortable old shoe. He had always been a practical joker, so he relished participation in the team's mock battles with water pistols. He made a special point of squirting the veteran backfield ace, Lenny Moore.

Because he wore thick glasses off the field (even though he didn't need them during a game) Bubba's eyes were checked.

"Doc," he drawled with a twinkle, "there's nothing wrong with my eyes. They just haven't caught up to the rest of my growth."

The one man who was not overly impressed by Bubba was the third Smith, Billy Ray, who was nicknamed "The Rabbit." He was the player Bubba was supposed to replace at tackle. Billy Ray wasn't going to let the rookie—or anybody else—take his job away. "If he beats me, we'll have a fantastic team," he said. "He's got to be better than I've heard. I've got experience, and that's worth gold in this league."

Certainly, Bubba was a big man who might be able to reach up and deflect a pass even before it crossed the line of scrimmage. But according to Billy Ray, the only thing the Colts were getting by using the rookie was "instant size."

Nevertheless, Bubba was in the line-up as the

Colts took on the Boston Patriots in an inter-
league exhibition game. His individual opponent was a good lineman named Lennie St. Jean.
Afterward, when St. Jean was asked his opinion
of Bubba, the Boston player had high praise.

After knocking down Patriot lineman Lennie St. Jean (60), Smith looks for the ballcarrier.

"I'd say he's as good as some guys who've been playing three or four seasons," he said. "You don't teach a man overnight to hit the way he hits."

But St. Jean also pointed out some flaws in

Bubba's play. "He's got a lot of good moves, but he's not as rough as he could be. Sometimes he beat me, but other times he showed a lack of experience."

What he was pointing out was something Baltimore coaches had also noted. Upon occasion, Bubba would crash through the line so intent on tackling the quarterback that he would allow himself to be sideswiped by the offensive center. A more experienced lineman would have been able to avoid being stopped in this manner. Yet, in a way, it was a natural mistake for a rookie to make. For tackling the quarterback always gives a lineman the same feeling that a halfback experiences when he scores a touchdown.

In the next game against the St. Louis Cardinals, Bubba did not play well. At least he didn't think so. He was repeatedly fooled by traps and draw plays. Not only did he bruise his knee, but he felt he had done nothing to help the team. The Colts lost by a score of 9-5.

But Coach Shula kept him in the line-up. There was only one way his rookie could get experience, and that was to play every minute of every game.

The fourth game of the season, against the Washington Redskins, proved to be a kind of reverse turning point in Bubba Smith's career as a pro-football player. He was matched against experienced Vince Promuto, and the Redskin lineman was able to handle him nicely, in spite of his 55-pound disadvantage in weight. Furthermore, Bubba was hit hard and he limped off the field with an injured knee.

Bubba sits on the bench while Colt trainers tend to his injured knee.

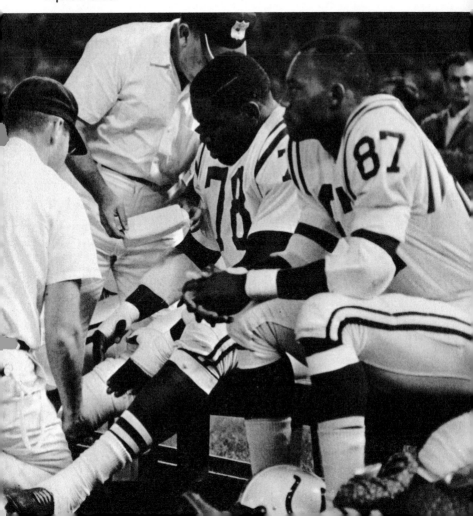

At first it was thought that the injury was minor. Bubba was expected to return to the line-up very soon. But then the knee swelled. It was bound in bandages and Bubba rested it. But as soon as the bandages were removed the knee swelled again.

Given the opportunity to play, Billy Ray Smith made the most of it. Perhaps it was the knowledge that Bubba would soon be on his feet again that made The Rabbit do such a good job. Now that he was playing again, he didn't care if the rookie sat on the bench forever, nursing his wounded pride.

At that point Bubba Smith began to doubt himself. He had been given every opportunity to make the grade, but he had not measured up to his full potential. Other, less publicized defensive rookies had broken into the pro ranks with a splash. Alan Page, who had also played in the 1967 Michigan State-Notre Dame tie game, was having a very successful season with the Minnesota Vikings. Perhaps, thought Bubba, he should gain a few more pounds. Maybe he would be more effective at 290 or 295. Of course, he might lose some of his speed that way.

Not until a November game against the Atlanta Falcons did Bubba get the chance to play again. Billy Ray had been slightly injured, and the coaches thought a rest would do him no harm, especially at the relatively advanced age of 32.

Back in his spot at left tackle, Bubba played a great game, even though he knew that he would be back on the bench when Billy Ray was ready to return. Bubba had profited from his previous mistakes and this time he was steady and less apt to be fooled. On three occasions he broke through the line and singlehandedly tackled the Falcon quarterback for a loss.

Then, as Bubba had expected, Billy Ray recovered and returned to his position. After that, Bubba watched from the sidelines as the Colts went on to tie Los Angeles for first place in the Coastal Division of the Western Conference.

By the end of the 1967 season, Bubba Smith was ready to admit that he had a lot to learn, and that in itself was a victory. He had already learned that the pros certainly were tough enough to hurt him badly when they caught him off guard. And they were smart enough to make him seem foolish when he allowed himself to be caught by traps, draw plays and the hundred other tricks the pros have up their sleeves.

He had also learned not to worry about his mistakes. He realized that, if he spent all his time

During a game with the Rams, Smith closes in on running back Tommy Mason, who has just taken the hand-off from Roman Gabriel.

By the end of the 1967 season Bubba Smith had shown just enough of his potential to make the N.F.L. aware of his presence.

brooding about them, he would get so discouraged that improvement would be impossible. And he had come to know how difficult it is for a player to sit on the bench and watch, feeling that he contributes nothing to the team.

Bubba had also shown just enough of his potential to make the rest of the N.F.L. aware of his presence. One veteran remarked, "I'd hate to be around when that guy starts playing the way I know he can!"

Even Billy Ray Smith, the man who had beaten back Bubba's challenge, had words of encouragement to offer.

"Mark my words," he said. "Bubba's day will come. And when it does he'll prove what everybody has always thought—even me. Bubba Smith can be a great one."

THE COMEBACK OF A ROOKIE
PAUL WARFIELD

When Paul Warfield began playing football at First Street Grammar School in Warren, Ohio, he weighed exactly 72 pounds. Slender, with thin arms and legs, he looked as if a good stiff wind might blow him off his feet. But there was little chance that the youngster would get hurt, for he played on a touch football team. Blocking was permitted, but not tackling.

Young Paul tried out as a quarterback, but the boy simply did not have a strong enough arm to

Carrying the ball for Warren Harding High, Paul Warfield tries to outmaneuver a group of enemy tacklers.

throw the long passes. Then he switched over to the end position and did quite well.

When the youth entered junior high school he wanted to try out for the football team, but his mother refused to give permission. She would not allow her son, whose weight had increased to only 95 pounds, to be roughed up by bigger boys. So, instead of running around a football field, he delivered newspapers for two years.

Paul's father, who was employed by Republic Steel, wanted to be able to boast of his son's athletic abilities to his co-workers. He understood why the boy wanted desperately to play football, for Mr. Warfield had played the guard position in high school in Tennessee. Paul and his

father began to pester Mrs. Warfield, asking her when she would consent to Paul's playing. Finally, she agreed that when Paul reached 130 pounds he could go out for football.

By that time he was ready to enter Warren Harding High School. And, in spite of the fact that he had never played tackle football in his life, Paul made the team.

Moreover, he blossomed out as a star in other sports. The teen-ager won letters in baseball, basketball and track, as well as football. He set the Ohio record for the 180-yard low hurdles, and the school broad jump record of 23 feet 9 inches.

Young Warfield was only 16 years old when

he was graduated from Warren Harding High. On the basis of his all-around athletic ability, he received offers from 67 colleges. Two Ohio State graduates who lived in Warren, Dr. Clyde Muter and Dr. Joseph Logan, talked him into attending their alma mater. When they pointed out that Ohio State had always had good track teams, Paul was convinced that it was the place for him.

At O.S.U. Paul continued to shine in a number of sports. He won two letters as a sprinter and broad jumper. In an N.C.A.A. meet, he placed second in the broad jump with a leap of 26 feet.

He was a fine center fielder, too, and played a great deal of amateur baseball. In fact, he was so good that some major league scouts contacted him

Competing in a college track meet, Warfield snaps the tape in the high-hurdle race.

and made him offers, but Paul refused to start at the Class-D level.

Besides, football had become his primary interest. And, in many ways, Paul Warfield's college football career was truly remarkable. Weighing 188 pounds and standing 6-feet 1-inch tall, Paul could play any position that did not require very much weight and brute strength. He shone on offense and defense. On offense, he played left halfback and split end. When the offensive team left the field he remained and moved into the defensive backfield.

On pass defense Paul was outstanding. In 1962 he was assigned to cover two of the top receivers in the country, Pat Richter of Wisconsin and Paul Flatley of Northwestern. He guarded them so well that they were almost helpless.

Richter went on to sign with the Washington Redskins and Flatley with the Minnesota Vikings. Warfield's tremendous coverage of Flatley seems all the more amazing considering the fact that, during the following year, defensive halfbacks on pro teams couldn't do much to stop the former Northwestern ace. In his first year with the Vikings, Flatley caught 51 passes for 867 yards, and was named the National Football League's Rookie of the Year.

Warfield sparkled as a running back, too. Buck-

Paul Warfield is brought down by Indiana tackler Woody Moore.

eye coach Woody Hayes did not rely on a passing attack to gain yardage. He liked to keep the ball on the ground. Other coaches throughout the country described the Ohio State offensive strategy as "five yards and a cloud of dust." And the lad from Warren, Ohio, was the mainstay of that running game.

Despite his lack of weight, in three years of rugged Big-Ten varsity play, Warfield carried the ball 191 times for 1,047 yards and a 5.5-yard average. He also scored eight touchdowns. His longest run from scrimmage was a 75-yard touchdown sprint that beat Indiana, 10-7.

And, although Hayes didn't believe in passing very much, whenever Ohio State threw the ball, Warfield was generally the one who caught it. In his college career he caught 39 passes, good for 525 yards and six more touchdowns. In his senior year he was State's top receiver, with 22 receptions worth 266 yards.

Even when he didn't have the ball, defenses were forced to keep an eye on him as he raced downfield. He scared them. For almost every time he went out on a "fly" pattern, he would get behind the defenses and into the clear. Had the quarterback thrown to him more often, his touchdown record would have been far more impressive.

Furthermore, he could be counted on when the chips were down and his team needed a score, even if the whole defense was ganging up on him. During his senior year, in a game against Michigan, Paul went out for a pass and found himself surrounded by Michigan jerseys. With a sudden burst of speed he tore past two defenders, whirled, leaped high and fell into the end zone clutching the ball. The 35-yard touchdown pass was completed with only 40 seconds left in the first half and helped spark the Buckeyes to a 14-10 victory.

Because of his tremendous speed Warfield was also part of Ohio's kickoff-return squad.

Warfield races for a touchdown against Michigan. The extra leg in the picture belongs to a Michigan player.

Once he got up a full head of steam, he seemed like a phantom as he breezed through the clutching arms of opposing players. In one season Paul returned 15 kickoffs for a total of 383 yards—almost 26 yards per return.

In all categories, Warfield gained 2,494 yards in his college career. Of course, Paul took a lot of punishment in the process. Many times he was hit by 250-pound defensive ends or tackles, and he usually had plenty of bruises to show the trainer after a game was over. But he could take the rough treatment. In his three seasons with the varsity, Warfield didn't miss a single game, and led the Ohio State team in total playing time. He was on the field for 373 minutes as a junior and 386 as a senior.

By the time he was graduated, Warfield had received several football honors. He had been named to the All Big-Ten squad in 1962 and 1963, and to the *Time* All-America team in 1963. He had also been chosen to play in the College All-Star game, the East-West game and the Hula Bowl game.

There was one other honor bestowed upon Paul Warfield that had nothing to do with football, but it was one he was particularly proud of. When he was 19 years old the intelligent, soft-spoken young man had been selected

Playing defense for Ohio State, Warfield breaks up a pass during the 1963 East-West game.

for a spot on the United States track team that would compete against a visiting Russian squad. He was chosen because of his 26-foot broad jump. At a party for the two teams Paul made a fine speech, which was warmly received. He expressed pride in his country and welcomed the Russian athletes to the competition. Later, he managed to place third in his event.

Long before his graduation, Paul had decided that he wanted to play pro football. On the basis of his record, he knew that he would be selected by some team, but he wasn't sure which one it would be. All he could do was wait.

During the 1964 college draft, the Cleveland Browns had to wait, too. Because of their record the year before, they had to stand by while the names of 10 outstanding players were called before they could make known their number-one choice. Blanton Collier, the new head coach of the Browns, knew which man he wanted, and the call came loud and clear. "The Cleveland Browns choose Paul Warfield of Ohio State University."

The Browns went on to pick other players in the draft: Billy Truax, defensive end, L.S.U.; Don Shackelford, tackle, University of the Pacific; Leroy Kelly, halfback, Morgan State. In all they selected over 20 top-ranked college athletes. Some of them would become members of the team and others would fail to measure up in the tryouts and would be sent on their way. But the Browns' first choice was considered a sure bet to make the team.

Warfield had also been drafted by the Buffalo Bills, of the American Football League. But he turned down their offer.

Later, Warfield learned that the Browns had not scouted him very much at all. Cleveland's player personnel-director, Paul Bixler, had seen him play in college exactly three times, once in each of his varsity years. Paul had done nothing spectacular in any of those games. But Bixler had been watching how the other side reacted to Warfield. He had seen them panic every time the Ohio star took off and raced downfield. He had noticed that the defense had shifted over to Paul's side of the field on almost every play. If the rough, tough Big-Ten was afraid of Paul Warfield, the kid must have something, he had thought.

Because of Coach Hayes' devotion to the running game, Bixler hadn't seen much of the rookie's receiving ability, either. But he had seen Warfield catch passes in high school, and knew that the boy could hold on to the ball.

For Coach Collier, however, Warfield presented a problem. Now that he had the rookie, what was he going to do with him? At first the Browns thought that Warfield should be used on defense. Their veteran mainstay on pass defense, Jim Shofner, was retiring. Because Warfield had been the top defensive back in his conference, he might be able to replace Shofner. But Paul had a slender build and weighed only 188 pounds. As a result, it seemed unlikely he would be able to take the pounding he would receive at the hands of big downfield blockers or bruising fullbacks.

He could certainly play the safetyman position. But, in a way, that would be a waste of a first-draft choice.

The Browns considered putting him in the flanker-back position. But flankers were often called upon to block, and the thought of the slim Warfield crashing into a rugged linebacker wasn't very appealing to Collier.

The tight-end position was also a possibility, but the drawback there was similar to the one that made the Browns think twice about making Warfield a flanker—tight ends blocked, too.

Pro football had long ago abandoned the use of running backs as light as Warfield, so he wasn't even considered for such a role.

Although the Browns were undecided about

what to do with the rookie, they had no doubts about having drafted him in the first place. Their choice had been based on sound reasoning.

Warfield was a natural all-around athlete. He was shifty and fast (having run the 100-yard dash in 9.6 seconds). And he had the indefinable quality that all stars have—"desire."

Paul Warfield was also a perfectionist. He never stopped practicing until he could do a thing the right way. He was the kind of person who would eat his heart out when he made an error. The Browns felt that, with a fellow like Warfield, strength and weight might not be very important.

If the Browns had any doubts about where Warfield belonged, he dispelled them immediately after reporting to training camp.

Blanton Collier had lined up his rookies in two groups. One group was assigned to run out to receive passes while the other defended. Then the players would switch assignments. This provided an opportunity for the Cleveland coach to get a close look at his number-one rookie.

Warfield ran just one pass pattern, and Collier and his assistants could hardly believe their eyes. The lad was a natural receiver. The word defense was immediately forgotten as far as the rookie was concerned.

Just to make sure they weren't kidding themselves, they put Warfield through his maneuvers again and again. They were amazed at what he could do. He had moves, speed, good hands and a fine change of pace, which would undoubtedly improve with experience. Paul Warfield became a regular receiver for the Cleveland Browns immediately after that first afternoon of practice.

Now a different problem arose. Which receiving position would he fill? Johnny Brewer was at tight end, Gary Collins at flanker and Rich Kreitling at split end. Who was going to make way for Warfield?

Brewer, who weighed 235 pounds and was a competent blocker, was an excellent receiver when it came to short passes. Warfield weighed only 188 and obviously wasn't equipped to handle frequent blocking chores. Besides, his speed would be wasted on short passes. He would be much more effective for the long "bombs."

Flanker Collins, standing 6 feet 4 inches tall, had the kind of height so important for a good receiver, plus the speed that enabled him to go deep and outrun many of the league's defensive backs. Warfield might be a step quicker, but Collins was certainly fast enough and could handle the blocking. So Collins had to stay where he was.

Kreitling had been Cleveland's number-one draft choice in 1959. In five seasons with the club, the former University of Illinois star had caught 102 passes, good for 1,590 yards and 15 touchdowns. He performed well on short passes, but was not as fast as Warfield or Collins.

The Cleveland coaching staff reasoned that, with Collins operating on one side and Warfield on the other, the team would pose a double threat on the long passes. At the same time, Johnny Brewer and the two backfield men (the halfback and fullback) could take care of the shorter ones. Warfield, therefore, had to play split end. By the process of elimination, Kreitling became expendable. He was traded.

Warfield's progress in training camp was outstanding. He continued to improve during exhibition games, showing the ability to get under the long passes thrown by Frank Ryan, the Browns' quarterback. By the time of the regular-season opener against the Washington Redskins, he felt he was ready to give a good account of himself.

However, Cleveland won the game without much help from their rookie hotshot. Paul did not catch one of the four passes that Ryan threw

The Redskins' Lennie Sanders (40) and Paul Krause (26) break up a pass to Warfield.

his way. Two were intercepted when the fledgling split end allowed defensemen to leap in front of him and steal the ball.

Perhaps Warfield was too nervous. Only the day before he had been married to a pretty girl named Beverly Keys. But he was not the sort of person who offers excuses for his mistakes. Afterward, veteran defensive-backfield ace Bernie Parrish tried to console his teammate. He told Warfield that he mustn't quit on himself just because of one bad game—he had to regain his old confidence.

Although Warfield was the kind of player who responded to encouragement, he was also a perfectionist. He realized that Parrish meant well and was trying to help him, but he also knew that he had to solve his problem by himself. In this frame of mind he began to practice almost endlessly. He watched movies of ball games. He listened to his coaches' advice. And he began to see the many things he was doing wrong.

First of all, he discovered that he was too anxious. In effect, he was trying to run with the ball before he had caught it.

Second, he had to time his pass cuts better. Instead of running eight to 12 yards before making his moves, he was running only five to six. Again, that showed he was overanxious.

Third, when he had watched films of previous games played by Cleveland, he had paid too much attention to the pass receivers on the other teams. He had been studying how they caught the ball and ran with it. Instead, he should have concentrated more on the defensive men who would be guarding him. Warfield had to observe how they moved their feet, what sort of fakes fooled each corner halfback or safetyman. He had to learn how to spot a defensive man's weakness and take advantage of it.

Fourth, he had to learn how to "catch the ball in a crowd." Defensive players obviously weren't going to stand around and give him room, admiring the splendid way he caught the football. Their job was to go after it, too. It was his job to outjump and outfight them for possession of the ball.

Fifth, he had to cut down on his jumping. Although Paul's powerful, heavy thighs enabled him to jump higher than almost anybody in the league, he was often going up into the air when he didn't have to—especially when he caught the ball stomach-high.

In this connection, the coaches pointed out that when a man is in the air he loses momentum. When he comes back to the ground, it takes him an extra second or two to regain his running speed. In that space of time a defensive man can race over and tackle him. Thus the extra second can make the difference between a long gain and a touchdown.

Sixth, Paul had to learn that sheer speed was not enough to get him past a defender. Many men who were faster than he was had failed to make the grade because they could not control their speed with a deceptive change of pace. On the other hand, many receivers who were slower than Warfield had succeeded with pro teams because they knew how to take advantage of the speed they possessed.

Seventh, even though Paul had learned a great many good moves and fakes with his head, shoulders and hips, he had to add more. And he had to use them in his pass cuts.

Warfield was an intelligent young man, so he learned quickly. Soon he began to show that he could execute what he had learned. And, as he improved in every department, quarterback Ryan placed more confidence in him.

In the Browns' second game, a tie with the St. Louis Cardinals, Warfield caught three passes for 63 yards. In the victory over the Philadelphia Eagles, Paul had six receptions for 97 yards. Against Dallas, a game the Browns also won, he snared five throws for 123 yards and three TDs.

It wasn't long before every team in the league was talking about the great Cleveland aerial attack. Collins operated on the right and Warfield on the left, and the pair of speedsters occasionally crossed paths to further confuse the enemy. The result was the Browns' best receiving combination since the old days, when Dante Lavelli and Mac Speedie had driven the opposition crazy.

After his team lost to the Browns, Dan Bishop of Dallas paid grudging tribute to Warfield. He said that perhaps the Cleveland flash wasn't capable of beating a defense all day, but he certainly could beat any cornerback or safetyman in the league at least once during the course of a game.

As soon as Warfield began to gather in Ryan's passes regularly, the enemy defenses began to double-team him. Paul didn't mind. In fact, he welcomed it, for the presence of two defenders forced him to "improvise" new moves and fakes that he might not have had the opportunity to use if he was facing only one man. On one occasion he made a 40-yard touchdown catch that caused the two men guarding him to blink in bewilderment.

In the huddle, Warfield had been ordered to run a "hook-shake" pattern. He faked to the out-

With a Lion defender clinging to his arms, Warfield leaps into the air for a pass.

side, but the smart defense didn't fall for that move, so the speedy end changed direction and moved toward the middle. Quarterback Frank Ryan, thinking that Warfield was going to keep on running in that direction, threw toward the middle of the field. However, just as the ball left the passer's hand, Warfield changed direction again and started back toward the outside. Looking back over his shoulder, he saw that the pass was now behind him. But the rookie was able to stop, turn on a dime, reach back, grab the ball and race away for the score.

Warfield received special tutoring in the fundamentals of blocking from another former great Cleveland receiver, Ray Renfro. He tried to show the rookie something about downfield blocking. But, although Warfield tried hard, he simply didn't have the power to put a dent in the bigger men. Once he tried to execute a block against linebacker Maxie Baughan, but Warfield just bounced off him like a rubber ball. However, he was able to learn how to block out enemy safetymen, who were usually not too much heavier or about the same weight.

Blanton Collier and the other Cleveland coaches likened the team of Collins and Warfield in football to a pair of home-run hitters in baseball. Just as the sluggers in baseball could hit the

Because of their ability to catch the long "bombs," Paul Warfield and Garry Collins posed a double threat to enemy defenses.

ball over an outfield fence and break up a ball game, Collins and Warfield could streak down-field and gather in the 50 and 60-yard touchdown passes that often snatched victory from defeat.

And because the two receivers had this ability, the defenses could not afford to play close to them. Just as baseball outfielders played back near the fence when the sluggers came to bat, football defenders had to play deeper when fast, sure-handed receivers were crouching down ready to take off and fly.

This helped to make the short passes doubly effective. Since the safetymen were forced to play back, the only men protecting the middle of the field were the slower linebackers, whom both Collins and Warfield could easily outrun. And, if the three linebackers ganged up on those two receivers, they faced the possibility that tight end John Brewer would show up out in the open. And Brewer was no slouch when it came to catching Ryan's passes.

The threat of a good passing attack made the ground attack harder to stop, especially when it was spearheaded by a man like the great Jimmy Brown. To add to the defenders' miseries, Brown was also a very slick pass receiver. So was half-back Ernie Green.

Although Warfield had been told to stay on the ground when a leap wasn't necessary, nobody ever told him to stop jumping altogether. When he took off on his springy legs he seemed to be floating. One alert photographer managed to snap a picture that showed Warfield leaping so high that his belt buckle was even with a defensive man's head. His style caused one imaginative Baltimore sportswriter to describe him as being "part Ray Berry, part Lenny Moore and part kangaroo."

As the season rolled on, the Cleveland Browns made a strong bid for the Eastern Division championship. Through their first 10 games, only the 33-33 tie with the Cardinals and a 23-7 upset at the hands of the Pittsburgh Steelers marred their record. The Browns were leading the Division handily.

Then they met the dangerous Green Bay Packers, who snapped the Browns' four-game winning streak. However, Warfield had his best day of the season against the Packers. He was all over the field, and even the powerful Packer defense was forced to put two men on him because he was beating their man-to-man defense to shreds. That day Paul caught seven passes worth 126 yards and scored two touchdowns. One of his scoring strikes covered 48 yards, the other 19. Green Bay managed to come out ahead, however, beating the Browns, 28-21.

"Mildly sensational," said Green Bay coach Vince Lombardi after the game. "That boy sure can jump."

After their defeat at the hands of the Packers, Cleveland quickly got back on the winning track with a 38-24 victory over Philadelphia. That meant they would have a chance to clinch the Eastern Division title when they met the second-place Cardinals the following week. Unfortunately the hard-driving St. Louis club knocked off Cleveland by a score of 28-19.

Even after the defeat, however, Blanton Collier's men led the Division by a slender margin.

Warfield eludes two Green Bay tacklers.

In order to win the title they had only to win their final game of the season against the New York Giants, the team with the worst record in the league.

But nobody in the Cleveland organization considered the Giant game a pushover. Team standings didn't mean a thing whenever the two teams tore into each other. Theirs was a traditionally bitter rivalry. Only the previous season, before their skid to the bottom because of injuries, the New Yorkers had beaten the Browns in the closing moments of the season's final game to win the Division championship.

Spurred on by the memory of that defeat, the Browns played an excellent game. As the first half drew to a close they led, 17-7. But they didn't consider that a safe margin. For, even though Giant quarterback Y. A. Tittle was old and slow, there was always something different in his bag of tricks. In the past he had often found new ways to beat his opponents. If there was any passer the Browns feared, it was old "Colonel Slick," as the sportswriters called him.

As a result, the Browns needed an "insurance" touchdown—before the half ended, if possible. That would give them a commanding edge and would break the morale of the badly battered Giants. The clock at Yankee Stadium showed that there were still 45 seconds left to play when Cleveland executed a surprise play to clinch the game and give them the championship. And the man most responsible for the success of the play was Paul Warfield.

The Browns' middle linebacker, Vince Costello, had managed to intercept a pass from Tittle over the middle of the line. Cleveland took possession of the ball on New York's 48-yard line. Then Frank Ryan called for a time-out and went to the bench to talk to Coach Collier.

"Warfield thinks he can beat Webb on a double-Z out," he said. "Is it all right with you if we try it?"

Collier agreed. "I think he can do it, too. Use the play."

The Browns' double-Z-out pass play required Warfield's greatest skill. He had to fake to the inside, break to the outside, make a long run upfield, then fake to the inside and break to the outside again. It was very tricky. Only an exceptionally fast man could make the play work.

As Warfield started to run his patterns Frank Ryan dropped far back to give the rookie time to make all the complicated moves. However, Warfield never did finish making them.

Defensive back Webb had been playing close to Warfield, trying to prevent him from catching

Ryan's deadly short passes. Warfield had been confident that once he got by Webb, he would have no trouble running away from him. He went through the first part of the play in fine style. He ran a fake to the inside, broke to the outside and began racing upfield. That was the first half of the double-Z out. But, as he started to sprint in a straight line, Webb just stood on the field, not knowing what the speedy rookie was up to.

When Warfield saw that Webb wasn't following him, he had no need for further faking. He just kept going and did not execute the second part of his moves. But now he had broken the pattern of the play. He wasn't sure Ryan would be able to figure out what he had in mind.

Warfield needn't have worried. Ryan was very glad to see that his receiver was in the clear. He threw an easy, floating pass, which Warfield plucked out of the air on the New York 10-yard line. He made it to within a yard of the goal line before he was stopped.

Seconds later, Ryan dropped another pass into the arms of Ernie Green. Cleveland had the additional touchdown it needed. They were to add a few more later in the game, but to all intents and purposes the game was over right then and there.

After the game the regular season was over, too. As sportswriters realized what Warfield had accomplished in his rookie year, they began to heap praise on him. They called him the best rookie receiver to come along in the past 10 years. A look at the records showed that he was the second-best receiver ever to wear the Cleveland Browns' uniform. He had caught 52 passes, many of them in real clutch situations. They were good for a total of 920 yards and nine touchdowns. The longest pass he caught covered 62 yards. It was also the longest pass Frank Ryan had completed that year.

Of all Cleveland's great receivers—past and present—only Mac Speedie had beaten that total, and he had done so four times. Warfield had outshone all of the others—Dante Lavelli, Ray Renfro, Darrell Brewster, Bobby Mitchell and Gary Collins. On top of that, those receivers had also had the benefit of Otto Graham's passing talent. Of course, Frank Ryan was a fine quarterback, but "the peerless Otto" was one of the greatest passers ever to step onto a football field. He was later elected to the football Hall of Fame. It is interesting to speculate on what Warfield might have accomplished with Graham throwing the ball.

Without a doubt, Paul Warfield's first season

had been an outstanding success. It had been a very good year for several other rookies, too. In fact, three of them managed to win individual championships. Newcomer Paul Krause of the Washington Redskins led the league in interceptions by plucking 12 enemy passes out of the arms of intended receivers. First-year man Bobby Walden of the Minnesota Vikings took the N.F.L. punting title away from perennial winner Yale Lary of the Detroit Lions by exactly one-tenth of a point. Walden averaged 46.4 yards per punt. And the kickoff-return leader was New York Giant freshman Clarence Childs, another young man with blazing speed. He won with 29.0 yards per return. On one kickoff, he had run 100 yards for a touchdown.

But none of these first-year men was selected as Rookie of the Year. That honor fell to a great running back named Charley Taylor, who also played for the Redskins.

Paul Warfield hadn't come out on top in any department, but that didn't bother Coach Collier. His rookie had come through in a big way. Warfield had made the Cleveland passing game one of the most dangerous in pro football. Furthermore, he showed signs of considerable improvement. At the end of the season, defensive coaches in the N.F.L. heaved a weary sigh and began trying to figure out how they could stop the flashy receiver. Maybe the answer was to keep giving him double-coverage, they thought. If they surrounded him wherever he went, they might keep him from breaking up games.

In the N.F.L. championship that year, the Baltimore Colts learned to their sorrow that assigning two or three men to guard Warfield *wasn't* the answer. Because the Colts were covering the Cleveland split end so heavily, Collins was out in the clear most of the time. So Ryan switched his attention to Collins and the fleet flanker caught three touchdown passes. The Browns knocked off the Colts, 27-0. Warfield didn't mind who scored the touchdowns, as long as his team won. For he knew that his mere presence had played a great part in the victory.

Then, in the All-Star game of 1965, disaster struck Warfield. The game is usually played at night. The lights at Soldier's Field in Chicago, where the contest is held, are not always in good order. And that was the basic reason for Warfield's injury.

In the first quarter, Cleveland had the ball on its own 24-yard line, third down, six yards to go. In the huddle Ryan called for a long pass to Warfield. As the Browns' split end took off, he found that defensive back Al Nelson (who was scheduled to report to the Philadelphia Eagles after the game) was sticking to him like glue. Warfield put on a burst of speed and managed to get a step ahead of Nelson. But when he looked up to see where the ball was, the light was so poor that he couldn't locate it. He had to stop for a moment so that he could find out where it was. That cost him the step he had gained.

Then Warfield spotted the ball. So did Nelson. Both men leaped high. As they crashed to the ground, Warfield's left arm was pinned under his body and Nelson fell across Paul's legs. Nelson got up. Warfield did not.

The Cleveland receiver was holding his arm at a peculiar angle as he was helped off the field. It was easy to see that the injury was serious. He was rushed to the hospital immediately.

X-rays showed that Warfield had a double fracture of the clavicle (also called "the collarbone"), which is the bone connecting the shoulder blade with the breast bone. An operation would be necessary to repair the damage.

As it turned out, two operations were necessary. A pin was inserted in the collarbone to promote healing, and the bone was wired together.

Paul Warfield was a worried man. He began to wonder whether or not his football career was over. Even if his arm healed, he might never be able to play again with his former skill; or he might be forced to run with his left arm swinging in a different way, which could slow him down.

The fractures were slow to heal. Finally one fracture mended itself, but the other did not. Time dragged by. Warfield fretted and fumed. But there was no way to hurry nature. There was nothing he could do but wait.

Finally, the doctor told him that the bones had knitted. The pin in his collarbone could be removed, but the wires would have to remain until sometime the following winter.

With the pin out of his arm, Warfield began to travel the long road back. And nobody was

Warfield strengthens his injured arm and shoulder by lifting weights.

sure he would make it, least of all Paul himself. First he ran a great deal in order to get his legs and wind back in shape. He did calisthenics and lifted weights to strengthen his injured arm and shoulder. Then he began to catch some soft passes thrown by his teammates. His body felt stiff and sore, especially in the shoulder area. After a while, he began to run some of his old pass patterns. He didn't perform too badly, but he was far from sharp.

The 1965 season got under way without Paul in the line-up. Walter Roberts had replaced him at end. Sometimes Clifton McNeil, who could play either flanker or end, would go in for Roberts. Or it might be Tom Hutchinson, a good receiver from the University of Kentucky.

Warfield worked out doggedly and kept setting dates when he might return to action. First he decided that he might come back for the fifth game of the season, which would be played against the Dallas Cowboys. When that proved to be impossible, he pushed the date one week ahead. Perhaps he might get into game number-six against New York. Then he switched to the seventh game against Minnesota.

The continual disappointments proved to be more than he could bear. He finally stopped giving himself a time limit. He would just keep plugging away until he was strong enough.

Deep in his heart Paul was wondering what would happen to him when he finally did get into a game. If somebody banged into his injured shoulder, it might be unable to stand the strain and the bone might splinter again, despite the wire holding it in place. The only way to find out was to play and see what happened.

To many superstitious people, the number 13 seems unlucky. To Paul Warfield it seemed to be just the opposite. For in the 13th game of the season, against the Los Angeles Rams, he trotted onto the gridiron to play football—exactly 128 days after his operation.

Warfield was wearing a special shoulder pad to protect the injury as much as possible. And he was warned to avoid blocking contact when it might be painful. His coaches felt that there was no use taking chances. The game itself didn't mean a thing because Cleveland had already clinched its second consecutive Eastern Division title. Both Warfield and the Browns found out about the injury that day. It had healed!

On the 10th play of the fourth quarter, after Paul had been playing for short periods of time and had caught three passes for a total of 30 yards, Ryan threw another pass his way. As the ball sailed through the air, three Rams rushed over to break up the play. Warfield, who had been racing upfield, stopped, turned and came back toward the pass. The three Rams were right on his heels.

As Warfield leaped high, one of the defenders hooked his injured arm, trying to break up the pass. The whole group went down in a heap, and the ball bounced loose for an incomplete pass. For a moment the Cleveland end remained in a sitting position, moving his arm and shoulder gently. Then he got up slowly and left the field.

In the dressing room his shoulder was examined. There was a lump in the area of his operation. But it didn't hurt very much. Nothing had "popped" out of place, either. X-rays showed later that the injury had not been aggravated by the rough treatment.

Just to be on the safe side, Warfield was kept out of the final game against St. Louis. But he did see considerable action against Green Bay in the N.F.L. championship game, which the Browns lost. That contest was played in very bad weather on a field that was covered with a film of mud and snow. Paul spent a good part of the time down on the ground, falling, slipping and sliding. But his shoulder held up under the punishment, and a few weeks later the wires were removed.

The former rookie sensation began his actual comeback in 1966. His shoulder felt healthy, but at times it stiffened up. He found that he was unconsciously favoring the injured area, and perhaps that was why he developed a "charley horse" in training camp.

Paul knew that the rest of the players were watching every move he made. For no one was sure how his injury would stand up under a full season of rugged football. His coaches were worried that a hard blow would open up the old incision. Throughout the practice season, Warfield's teammates found themselves holding their breath whenever he was tackled.

Though his comeback was slow, it was steady. Ryan didn't pass to him much during the first few games. But then he began to feed the ball to the split end more often. As Paul got back in the groove, he found that enemy defenses were paying him the supreme compliment—they were using two men to cover him. He knew that they respected him as a scoring threat once again. Warfield's recovery also meant that opposing teams had to contend with the formidable combination of Warfield on the left and Collins on the right, just as they had in Paul's rookie year.

In the final game of the 1966 season, Warfield

In the 1967 season, Warfield was a much improved down pass during the Century Division title game, despite daring interceptors.

player. In this sequence of pictures he snares a touch-
the efforts of Larry Wilson (8), one of the league's most

was the same player who had stood the league on its ear in 1964. He caught six passes for a total of 161 yards. Over the whole season he had 36 receptions for 741 yards and five touchdowns.

In 1967 Paul Warfield was a much-improved player. He was older, wiser in football lore and he could read the enemy's defenses better. Often, after a sprint over the chalk stripes, he would come back into the huddle and give quarterback Frank Ryan valuable tips on what the enemy might be planning and suggest plays he might call to cross them up.

That year the Cleveland Browns won the championship of the Century Division in the Eastern Conference by beating the St. Louis Cardinals by a score of 20-16. And Cleveland scored its first touchdown in the second period on a beautiful pass from Frank Ryan to Paul Warfield.

Glossary of Terms

(**Boldface** type indicates a cross reference.)

AUDIBLE (n.):   A color and a number shouted by the **quarterback** at the **line of scrimmage.** This tells his teammates to forget the play he called in the huddle and alerts them for a new play.

AUTOMATIC (n.):   Almost the same as **audible.** It is the new play for which the team has been alerted.

BLIND SIDE (n.):   Any area not in a player's line of vision. For example, if a player is looking to the right, his blind side would be to his left.

BLITZ (n.):   A defensive charge in which the **linebackers, corner halfbacks** and sometimes the **safetyman** rush across the **line of scrimmage,** attempting to tackle the **quarterback** or the **running back** who has the ball. (If the safetyman is also moving in, it is called a **safety blitz.**)

BOMB (n.):   A long forward pass which results in a big gain or a touchdown.

BOOTLEG (n.):   Hiding the ball on the hip or behind the thigh. This is done by a **quarterback** who fakes handing the ball to a **running back,** hides the ball in the manner described and runs or **rolls out** with the ball.

BUTTON
HOOK (n.):   A **pass pattern** in which the receiver runs out a few yards, then turns back to face the passer. The pattern is almost a hook-shaped figure.

CLIP (v.):   To block a player from behind, usually across the back of the legs. This is not legal and should not be confused with **blind-side** block, which is legal.

COFFIN
CORNER (n.):

The sidelines between the 10-yard line and the end zone at the extreme corners of the playing field.

COMEBACK
PASS (n.):

Similar to **button-hook** pass.

CORNER
HALFBACK (n.):

A **defensive halfback** who plays five to 10 yards behind the **line of scrimmage** and toward the sidelines, but not directly on the sidelines.

DEFENSE (n.):

The defending team; the team not in possession of the ball.

DEFENSIVE
HALFBACK (n.):

One of two men who line up six or more yards behind the **line of scrimmage.** Their primary duties are to guard against a forward pass.

DOUBLE-
TEAM (v.):

To guard one player with two opposing players.

DOWN AND
IN (n.):

A **pass pattern** in which the receiver runs out a few yards, then cuts across toward the middle of the field.

DOWN AND
OUT (n.):

A **pass pattern** in which the receiver runs a few yards, then cuts toward the sidelines.

DRAFT (n.):

The method of selecting college players in the pro football leagues. Under the rules of the draft, the team that has finished last the year before is allowed to choose a player ahead of every other team. The club that has won the championship picks last. This procedure allows the team with the poorest record to obtain the player it thinks best. When a new team is formed within a league, it may get "first-draft" rights.

DRAW PLAY (n.):

An offensive running play in which the **quarterback** drops back as if to pass and a backfield man sets himself as if to block. The charging defensive linemen are allowed to run close to the blocker. As the quarterback drops back he hands the ball to the player who was only pretending to block, and the ball carrier runs straight through the hole opened up by the fooled defensive players.

EATING THE
BALL (n.): An instance in which a **quarterback** allows himself to be tackled for a loss behind the **line of scrimmage**. He does this rather than try to throw a pass which might be intercepted.

END SWEEP (n.): A wide run around either end of the **line of scrimmage** by a **running back**.

FAIR CATCH (n.): A type of **punt** reception in which the receiver raises his arm over his head while the ball is still in the air to signal that he will not try to run with the ball when he catches it. He does this when he realizes he will be tackled the instant he gets the ball. If anyone on the kicking team makes contact with him, a foul will be called. A fair catch may be called only on a punt, *not* on a kickoff or a field goal attempt that falls short.

FLANKER
BACK (n.): An **offensive halfback** who is stationed about six or seven yards away from the other backfield men. He is used mostly to catch passes, to block or to fool the defense into thinking he will catch a pass.

FLARE PASS (n.): A pass thrown to a backfield man who is moving toward the sidelines behind the **line of scrimmage.**

FLAT ZONE (n.): A part of the field of play between the offensive ends and the sidelines, behind the **line of scrimmage.** A **flare pass** is thrown into this area.

FLY (n.): A **pass pattern** in which the receiver runs straight downfield as fast as he can, without faking or cutting, in an attempt to run past all the defensive players.

FREE SAFETY (n.): A defensive back playing very deep. He doesn't cover any offensive player in particular, but is "free" to help anyone in the defensive backfield who needs help. He is often stationed on the **weak side.**

FRONT FOUR (n.) : The two defensive ends and the two defensive tackles.

FULLBACK (n.) : An offensive backfield player usually stationed four yards behind the quarterback; a powerful ball carrier who can plunge into the line and is able to block well.

GROUNDING THE BALL (n.) : An instance in which a **quarterback** finds his receivers covered and, rather than risk an interception or being tackled behind the **line of scrimmage,** he throws the ball where it can't be reached by his receivers, as well as opposing players. If an official rules that the ball was thrown in such a way that it would have been impossible for a receiver to catch it, a penalty is called on the play.

I-FORMA-TION (n.) : An offensive formation in which the **halfback, flankerback** and **fullback** (not necessarily in that order) line up in single file behind the **quarterback.**

INELIGIBLE RECEIVER (n.) : An offensive player who is not permitted to catch a forward pass. Only those players who are a yard or more behind the **line of scrimmage** (not counting offensive ends) are allowed to catch forward passes. Usually, only the ends and backfield men are eligible. This means that the center, the two offensive tackles and two offensive guards are ineligible.

IN MOTION (adj.) : Running behind the **line of scrimmage** while the **quarterback** is calling signals. If the movement is forward, a penalty will be called.

INSIDE (n.) : The area toward the middle of the field, between the two **defensive halfbacks** or corner linebackers.

INTERFER-ENCE (n.) : There are really two kinds of interference, one legal, the other illegal. An offensive player blocking for a teammate who is carrying the ball is "running interference" for the ball carrier, and that is legal. A player who pushes, shoves or otherwise hinders another player catching a pass is guilty of "illegal interference," which calls for a penalty. A player is also guilty of illegal interference when he interferes with an opposing player trying to catch a **punt.**

INTERIOR LINEMEN (n.):	The offensive center, offensive tackles and offensive guards.
KEEPER (n.):	Same as a **bootleg.**
LATERAL PASS (n.):	A pass made to the side or backward. If the ball is thrown forward, no matter how small the distance, it becomes a forward pass, even if the pass is executed behind the **line of scrimmage.**
LINE OF SCRIMMAGE (n.):	The imaginary line at which the two sets of linemen, offensive and defensive, face each other. It is established by the position of the ball.
LINEBACKER (n.):	A defensive player who is usually positioned about two or three yards behind the **line of scrimmage.** Normally there are three linebackers—a middle linebacker and two corner linebackers.
LOOK-IN PASS (n.):	A play in which the **quarterback** takes the snap from center, straightens up and throws a pass over the scrimmage line to an end or **flankerback** slanting toward the **inside.**
MAN-TO-MAN DEFENSE (n.):	An arrangement in which a defensive player tries to cover an offensive receiver by himself.
OFFENSE (n.):	The attacking team; the team in possession of the ball.
OFFENSIVE HALFBACK (n.):	A backfield ball carrier with more or less the same duties as a **fullback.** He is usually faster, but not as heavy as a fullback.

OFFSIDE (adj.): Illegally beyond the scrimmage line before the ball is snapped from center.

OPTION PLAY (n.): A ball carrier's play in which he has the choice of running with the ball or passing it to a receiver.

PASS PATTERN (n.): The running and faking movements of a receiver. Different teams have different descriptions for the same patterns. For instance, one team might use the term "square out" to mean a short dash straight ahead followed by a quick cut toward the sidelines. Another team might use the term "sideline pass" to mean the same thing.

PERSONAL FOUL (n.): An illegal act by one player against another, such as clipping, piling on, punching, kicking, grabbing a player's face mask, unnecessary roughness, etc. It calls for a 15-yard penalty.

PITCHOUT (n.): A short pass thrown laterally or backward to an **offensive halfback** or **fullback.**

PLACE KICK (n.): A type of kick for which a teammate holds the ball so that its point rests on the ground or a kicking tee. It is used when attempting a field goal or an extra point after a touchdown.

POCKET (n.): The protective arc around the **quarterback** formed by offensive players. They block opposing players while the quarterback prepares to throw the ball.

POWER SWEEP (n.): A run around the end of the **line of scrimmage** with plenty of **interference** to protect the ball carrier.

PUNT (v. and n.): To kick the ball to the opposing team. The ball is held by the kicker and, unlike a **place kick,** does not make contact with the ground before being kicked.

QUARTER-BACK (n.): The offensive player in the backfield who calls signals while crouched over the center. He does most of the passing.

QUARTERBACK
SNEAK (n.):
A **quarterback's** line plunge, designed to pick up one or two yards when a first down or touchdown is just a short distance away.

RED DOG (n.):
Same as a **blitz.**

REVERSE (n.):
A play that starts out one way, then reverses its direction and goes the other way through the process of a handoff.

ROLLOUT (n.):
A **quarterback's** maneuver in which he runs behind the **line of scrimmage** toward the sidelines before throwing a pass. It is used frequently in college, but not very often in pro football.

RUNNING
BACK (n.):
Either the **offensive halfback** or the **fullback.**

SAFETY (n.):
A two-point score that results from either tackling an offensive ball carrier behind his own end zone, forcing him out of bounds inside the 10-yard area of the end zone, or driving him back behind his end zone.

SAFETY
BLITZ (n.):
A **blitz** that includes the **safetyman** as part of the defensive charge.

SAFETYMAN (n.):
A defensive player, stationed toward the center of the field, who is the last line of defense. His primary job is guarding against passes.

SAFETY-VALVE
PASS (n.):
A play in which the **quarterback,** unable to find a receiver downfield who is unguarded, throws to a backfield man who has stayed close to him to block. The ball is thrown behind the **line of scrimmage.**

SCRAMBLER (n.):
A **quarterback** who runs out of the **pocket** and scurries about, trying to dodge defensive players while looking for someone to pass to.

SCREEN PASS (n.):
An offensive play in which the **quarterback** goes back to pass and then moves back even deeper as

opposing players are permitted to chase him. Meanwhile, two or more blockers move to one side. The quarterback throws a short pass behind the **line of scrimmage** to a receiver, who then gets behind the blockers and runs with the ball.

SHAKE (n.):
A **pass pattern** run by a receiver. It is a long, curving arc. Thus a "hook-shake" would be a "hook" pattern followed by a "shake" pattern.

SIDELINE PASS (n.):
A **pass pattern** in which the receiver runs out a few yards, then cuts sharply and moves toward the sideline.

SLOT (n.):
An open area in the **line of scrimmage,** between the **split end** and the offensive tackle.

SLOTBACK (n.):
An offensive backfield man, usually the **flanker back** but quite often the **running back,** who stations himself in the **slot** about a yard or two behind the **line of scrimmage.**

SPLIT END (n.):
A receiver, stationed on the **line of scrimmage** about five yards from the rest of the offensive linemen. His primary job is receiving passes and he does very little blocking.

STACK UP (v.):
To stop a ball carrier, either at the **line of scrimmage** or slightly behind it, as he attempts to plunge through the defenses.

STRONG SIDE (n.):
The side of the offensive line where the **flanker back** is stationed. Sometimes it also means the side where both the flanker back and **tight end** are stationed.

SUICIDE SQUAD (n.):
A special squad used on kickoffs.

SWING PASS (n.):
See **flare pass.**

TAXI SQUAD (n.): A group of players who belong to a team and practice with them, but are not on the team's official roster of players. They cannot play in league games unless they are taken off the taxi squad and placed on the official roster.

T FORMA-
TION (n.): An offensive formation in which the **quarterback** lines up directly behind the center, with the **fullback** a few yards behind him and set between two **halfbacks,** thus forming a T-shaped pattern. There are many variations of the basic T.

TIGHT END (n.): An offensive player, stationed on the **line of scrimmage,** who receives passes and helps with the blocking. Most of the time the tight end and **flanker back** are on the same side of the formation.

TOUCHBACK (n.): A situation in which a ball is out of play in the end zone. A touchback occurs when a team intercepts a pass in its own end zone or receives a punt and either lets it roll untouched or downs the ball in the end zone. No points are scored. The ball is brought out to the 20-yard line and put into play.

TRAP PLAY (n.): A play in which a defensive lineman or **linebacker** is allowed to penetrate the offensive team's backfield, and then is blocked from the side. Once called a "mousetrap" play.

TURN THE
CORNER (v.): To cut sharply around the end of the **line of scrimmage.**

WEAK SIDE (n.): The side of the offensive formation that the **flanker back** is *not* on.

ZONE
DEFENSE (n.): A pass defense in which defensive players guard assigned territory rather than individual pass receivers.

Index

Page numbers in italics refer to photographs.

About the Author

Howard Liss has seen pro football grow up and, at one time or another, has played nearly every major sport. He is the author of a number of books for children and has collaborated on books with such sports stars as Yogi Berra, Willie Mays, Fred "Curly" Morrison and Y. A. Tittle. Mr. Liss and his family live in New York City.